Race in the News

Also by Ian Law

Racism, Ethnicity and Social Policy
Local Government and Thatcherism
  (with H. Butcher, R. Leach and M. Mullard)
The Local Politics of Race
  (with G. Ben-Tovim, J. Gabriel and K. Stredder)
Race and Housing in Liverpool
Racial Disadvantage in Liverpool
  (with G. Ben-Tovim, V. Brown, D. Clay, L. Loy and
  P. Torkington)
A History of Race and Racism in Liverpool, 1660–1950
  (with J. Henfrey)

Race in the News

Ian Law

palgrave

First published 2002 by
PALGRAVE
Houndmills, Basingstoke, Hampshire RG21 6XS and
175 Fifth Avenue, New York, N. Y. 10010
Companies and representatives throughout the world

PALGRAVE is the new global academic imprint of St. Martin's Press LLC Scholarly and Reference Division and Palgrave Publishers Ltd (formerly Macmillan Press Ltd).

ISBN 0–333–74074–2 hardback
ISBN 0–333–74075–0 paperback

This book is printed on paper suitable for recycling and made from fully managed and sustained forest sources.

A catalogue record for this book is available from the British Library.

Library of Congress Cataloging-in-Publication Data
    Law, Ian.
    Race in the news/Ian Law.
      p. cm.
    Includes bibliographical references and index.
    ISBN 0–333–74074–2
      1. Mass media and race relations. I. Title.
P94.5.M55 .L38 2001
305.8—dc21   2001036526

10	9	8	7	6	5	4	3	2	1
11	10	09	08	07	06	05	04	03	02

Printed in China

Contents

List of Tables

Acknowledgements

This book developed from a research project funded by the Commission for Racial Equality which was concerned to examine the representation of race in the British news during the General Election of 1997. I would therefore like to thank the CRE for funding this project and for those CRE staff who have been involved in the development, implementation and dissemination of this research including Herman Ouseley, Colin Hann, Chris Myant, Greville Percival and Marjorie Thompson.

I would also like to thank my colleagues in the Institute of Communication Studies, David Morrison and Michael Svennevig, for their help and assistance with methodology and project design. Despite 'going my own way' in writing up the project, their help at an early stage was invaluable. In addition discussion with Paul Statham was particularly helpful.

In the massive task of data collection undertaken on the initial project, which covered 18 news sources, 7 days a week for 6 months, particular thanks go to technical staff in Communication Studies, the team of coders based in the Department of Sociology and Social Policy and particularly Bimal Bhanu for assistance in managing this task.

I have also been particularly lucky to have been working in a stimulating and supportive environment at Leeds, and here I would like to thank Malcolm Harrison, Carl Hylton, Debbie Phillips, Jo Goodey, Ray Pawson, Alan Deacon, Carol Smart, Kirk Mann, Max Silverman, Mick Gidley and all those associated with the Centre for Ethnicity and Racism Studies. Also, thanks to Marco Martinelli for encouraging my work on positive action through invitations to seminars in New York and Liege. Joint work with Malcolm Harrison and Max Silverman on the production of positive action papers contributed directly to Chapter 5 in this book, and many thanks to them for their cooperation. Thanks also to Dario Melossi for the opportunity to present and discuss material from Chapter 4 at an ISA conference at the University of Bologna, and for his comments. Thanks also to the unknown reviewers for their valuable comments. While in the USA completing this manuscript, I would also like to thank Jennifer Glass,

Mary Smith, Jim Price and Kevin Leicht at the Department of Sociology, University of Iowa for their kindness and assistance.

On a more personal note, this book could have not been completed without the love and support of Jude, in spite of her traumatic accident, and also Sebastian and Alexander. This book is particularly dedicated to Sebastian given his interest and aspirations in the world of journalism.

IAN LAW

The author and publishers wish to thank the following for permission to reproduce copyright material: Independent Television Commission for material from *Television: Ethnic Minorities Views*; and the Broadcasting Standards Commission for material form its *1991 Annual Survey*. Every effort has been made to contact all the copyright-holders. but if any have been inadvertently omitted the publishers will be pleased to make the neccssary arrangement at the earliest opportunity.

Introduction

Race-thinking is still a dominant form of social cognition across the globe. The allusions of blood, lineage, nation and ethnicity are brought together in different ways across most societies to construct particular populations or social groups as races. Despite a century of opposition to scientific, biological notions of race, for many people races are real, and these ideas invade and pervade global communications. In Europe, the symbolic representation of the peoples of the world as four different coloured races was embodied in their presentation as 38–ton plastic giants in the opening parade of the 1998 football World Cup in Paris. This provided a solid reminder to global viewers of the normality of such perceptions as they were shown to a huge television audience slowly clanking down the streets of the French capital. *The Times* captured this scene on its front page with a photograph of the yellow 'plastic oriental giant shuffling towards three counterparts' (10 June 1998). This use of the idea of race was reported unquestioningly by the world's media.

The durability and power of the race idea is based on the ways in which it makes sense of the world for people. It can provide an easy, if wholly inaccurate, label for physical, social and cultural differ-ence, it may provide a means of asserting superiority, purity and exclusion and it may also provide a platform for the assertion of justice, equality and related freedoms. In these ways, ideas of race have been mobilised to construct both racist and anti-racist ideas over many centuries. News organisations often draw on these ideas and use the lens of race extensively in reporting and portraying news events concerning nations, ethnic groups and, in particular, migrating groups. News media have been a key site for the representa-tion of ideas about racialised groups, providing a mass of comment, information and speculation which repeats, reinvents and shapes wider sets of race-related ideas. This book, and the research on which it draws, seeks to identify and evaluate how race is addressed in contemporary news coverage, with a particular focus on Britain and the USA.

The increasing significance of international migration, the engagement of major public institutions with issues of ethnic and cultural
diversity and the prevalence of violent racism are key features of
European and American societies at the beginning of the twenty-first
century. This book is concerned to examine the extent to which news
organisations are either obstructing or facilitating contemporary debates about these issues through representation of race news. Content
and discourse analysis of news material is used to assess shifts and
trends in the portrayal of issues of ethnic relations and migration,
which are frequently circumscribed by notions of race. This process
of racialisation needs to be subject to constant scrutiny and challenge.
Chapter 1 is concerned to address fundamental questions of the conceptualisation and meaning of racism and in particular to assess the
intellectual tools available to measure and evaluate racism in the
media.

In carrying out this critical task, however, it is also important to
have a grasp of overall patterns and trends in news coverage and
identify which issues receive privileged treatment and which issues
and voices are silent. Much analysis of the treatment of race in the
news has been too selective, lacking in empirical depth and therefore
inadequate in providing an assessment of the 'big picture' of the scale
and pattern of continuity and change. Global communications are a
rapidly changing environment and here we might expect to find rapidly
changing representations of race. This book does track significant
improvements in news coverage of ethnic relations, racism and migra-
tions since the 1980s as well as confirming persistent problems using
an intensive large-scale content analysis which is reported on in
Chapter 2.

The relatively optimistic message of this book needs to be set against
a wider context of political and policy failure in tackling racial discrimination, in reducing racial, ethnic and social inequalities and in halting
the rise of racial and ethnic violence across Europe and the USA in the
1990s. For example, in Britain recent estimates indicate that over a
quarter of a million people are likely to suffer from racial harassment
every year. The normality of racist behaviour is a continuing feature of
private family lives and domestic environments for many, as the police
video in the Stephen Lawrence Inquiry revealed. (Stephen Lawrence
was a black, 18-year-old, A-level student who was stabbed twice with a
weapon, similar to a kitchen knife, through the chest and arm as he
waited for a bus in Eltham, south-east London on 22 April 1993 by a

group of white youths. He ran 130 yards with a punctured lung and paralysed arm before bleeding to death.) The campaign and resulting inquiry into Stephen Lawrence's death was the most significant event in British debates over race in the 1990s (for the full Inquiry report see www.official-documents.co.uk/document/cm42/4262/). The case provided a platform for the mobilisation and reinvigoration of anti-racist ideas and voices in British society, and a set of significant legal and institutional changes with far-reaching effects are in the process of being implemented. Despite its centrality in British news investigated here it is a case which unfortunately is largely unknown by news audiences in the USA and in other European countries. Similarly, there have been many murders resulting from violent racism in these countries which are largely unknown in the UK. News coverage of the Lawrence case is examined in Chapter 4.

The pervasive impact of violent racism on the personal relationships, health and well-being of many continues to be immense. Further British evidence shows that one in six from minority ethnic groups suffer racial harassment at work, and one in four live in fear and anxiety about racial harassment generally. The casual and persisting pattern of racial discrimination in employment is well-established and Modood *et al.* (1997) recently found that one in five from minority ethnic groups has been refused a job for that reason.

Some of the reasons for the triple pattern of official failure to seriously challenge these issues need to be recognised. Firstly, inflated expectations that individual rights-based law could produce real reductions in group inequalities have been misplaced. Secondly, the fact that racism makes fundamental sense of the world for some people means that ideas and stereotypes have been much more impervious to intervention and change than was previously thought. The speed with which old ethnic and national antagonisms can be remembered, reinvigorated and fought for across the world parallels the problem of persisting racisms. Thirdly, poor understanding of the causes of, and patterns in, racial and ethnic inequalities has often produced poor policy, for example where 'anti-racist' strategies operate to reproduce new forms of social division and exclusion in practice. Fourthly, these problems have often been exacerbated by a failure of political, public service and elite leadership; with a tendency to push away the often difficult and embarrassing problems that race issues raise from the centre of attention and the focus of day-to-day concerns.

Partly because of the controversial character of race issues and also the central linkage of ideas of race to those of national identity, particularly in the British context, race has not been pushed away from the centre of concern by news organisations. On the contrary, a race element may be seen to give an added value to a news story particularly where it can be linked in some way to either crime or sex, or preferably both. The double movement of exposing racism and at the same time reinforcing racist linkages between race, violence and dangerousness in the coverage of crime news is also examined here. The intractable and worrying perpetuation of racism in news representation is the key focus for Chapter 3 with particular attention to issues of race and rape and migration. The extent to which this constitutes, for major news organisations, a 'collective failure to provide an appropriate and accessible service' is then the acid test of institutional racism.

Two key problems with the social and political construction of race provide a context for examining race news. Firstly, there is a general tendency across many fields to retain and speak through racial categories and racial meanings when addressing issues affecting minority ethnic groups. This 'playing with fire' may, at best, have a double-edged effect of challenging racial and ethnic inequalities as notions of race become further embedded in language and communication. Secondly, there is a further general tendency to evaluate, compare and measure many facets of social life against a white norm. This process of 'standardising whiteness' may be revealed in whitecentric decision-making across a huge range of institutional and organisational contexts as well as in much social policy and social research.

Differentiation in racial stereotyping, socio-economic position, migration history, educational attainment, political participation and perceptions of social citizenship are significant across minority ethnic groups and they are becoming increasingly evident (Law, 1996). Use of simplistic, inaccurate and misleading conceptions of their social location should be consistently rejected. The most recent large-scale study of minority ethnic groups in the UK (Modood *et al.*, 1997) highlights the divergence of socio-economic trajectories within and amongst these groups. Using data on earnings, unemployment and professional and managerial occupations as indicators of the extent of employment disadvantage it is evident that there is:

• severe and persistent disadvantage evident amongst Pakistani and Bangladeshi Muslims;

- relative disadvantage amongst Indians and Caribbeans; and
- with Chinese and African Asians having problems only in gaining access to top jobs in large organisations (1997: 65).

In terms of educational qualifications, Labour Force Survey data shows a complex pattern of attainment for Black Africans and Caribbean men and women with a different pattern evident at degree level, A-level and amongst those with no qualifications. There is no evidence here of homogenous black underachievement, far from it, on a variety of indicators African men come out on top, as for example this group have the lowest proportion of people with no qualifications. Apart from the diverging fortunes of different minority groups, there are increasing socio-economic divisions within minority groups. Data from the Policy Studies Institute (PSI) in Britain shows, for example, a trend of economic polarisation among young Caribbean men, and to some extent women, who are both among those with the highest average earnings, and amongst those with the highest rates of the unqualified and the unemployed. This pattern of diverging socio-economic inequality has particular implications for other aspects of life such as health. Nazroo's (1997) analysis shows higher levels of ill-health amongst Caribbeans, Pakistanis and Bangladeshis and a clear relationship with socio-economic status. This polarisation is also evident in housing where differences in income and wealth are a major factor in accounting for housing-market outcomes. Here we see the contradictory trends of increasing suburbanisation and increasing inner-city concentration happening at the same time although at different rates and in different areas across minority ethnic groups, and these patterns are likely to continue.

Forms of social and economic disadvantage are, then, frequently evaluated solely in relation to comparison with whites, and therefore racial categories are crucial here in the identification of patterns of ethnic inequality. In addition, increasing evidence of ethnic differences and inequalities within the white group, for example amongst the Irish or more recent migrants from Eastern Europe, means that using the white group as a yardstick for comparison is becoming increasingly problematic. The adequacy of this form of evaluation needs questioning as, for example, it may imply a broad policy concern with achieving minority ethnic representation in the labour market similar to that of the majority 'white' group. Here, then, difference is constructed as a policy problem. Clearly, a whole range of aspects of difference in, for example, educational and career aspirations, attitudes to self-employment or choice in the housing market exist across ethnic groups but to what extent are they appropriate for or amenable to policy intervention? The answer hinges on the meaning of the notion of equality and the ability to integrate issues of ethnic difference within this idea. This key problem in the construction of anti-racist ideas has also been identified by Lloyd (1994). She stresses the importance of engaging with the tensions between universalistic notions of equality and particularistic notions of cultural difference. Anti-racism is a key focus for discussion in this book and issues of conceptualisation and representation are addressed in Chapter 4.

Racial and ethnic inequalities in power and employment in news organisations have been subject to persistent criticism, as have policies of affirmative action, positive discrimination and positive action which seek to reduce employment inequalities. Chapter 5 assesses the state of positive action in Britain, its impact on news organisations and link-ages to changing patterns of representation. In considering the development of positive action, a framework of issues for practice are explored. Here, renewing the basis of justifiable arguments for the development of positive action strategies, in a relatively favourable political climate, is seen as a key challenge.

The eighteenth century saw Britain at the zenith of the European slave trade (Law 1981) and earlier looser fragments of racist mythologies came to cohere and appear in different forms of news communication. The nineteenth century saw the rise of liberal humanitarianism, scientific racism and the British Empire, and the full flowering of racist discourse influenced a vast range of forms of international communication. At the close of the twentieth century we are beginning to see the bones of racism being laid bare as racist discourse becomes more tightly circumscribed and the voices of minorities become stronger. In the twenty-first century, global communications will be a key site for the struggle between racist and anti-racist social forces. The freedom of racist communication is becoming greatly enhanced through the use of the internet and other new technologies, and new, dangerous and rapidly changing forms of racist expression are likely to emerge. In this context, the importance of mainstream news organisations to lead in promoting cultural diversity and anti-racism through responsible journalistic and editorial practice is of vital and increasing importance. In Britain such practice is beginning to dominate news organisations and this book is concerned to chart how far this 'anti-racist show' extends.

It is often the case that key texts and key experiences have a significant influence on the direction that a book takes. This text is no exception. *Policing the Crisis* (1978) by Stuart Hall and his colleagues provided an early set of signposts in the critical analysis and interpretation of news messages in the British context. My involvement with a collective of anti-racist activists and researchers in Liverpool (Merseyside Area Profile Group) who sought to operationalise such critical analysis in the investigation of a range of key social institutions including local news producers was also a key period in the formation of my ideas. The output from this group's research and campaigning activity is documented in *Racial Disadvantage in Liverpool* (1980). Here, pursuing change in the production of news was one key objective. One way in which this was pursued, given the intractability of local newspapers and television, was by the production of a glossy community-based magazine *Black Linx*. I worked as an editor on this magazine during my time at Merseyside Community Relations Council in the 1980s. Working on the production of news with a number of black colleagues provided valuable experience in the politics of both production and representation. We as media workers and community activists often wanted to focus on politics and policy, but an overwhelming request from readers was for the publication of poetry written by local people. This poetry often, but not always, engaged with reflections on racism, and sometimes local events, and was a request to which we happily agreed. Giving voice turned out to be more powerful and empowering for many readers than contesting the 'truth' of news coverage and engaging in debate over local politics and institutional racism.

This book also seeks to engage at a variety of points with American debates on race and the media and here two recent publications provided valuable benchmarks for contemporary analysis. John Gabriel's book *Whitewash* (1998), usefully brought together an investigation of whiteness with a grounded analysis of the politics of race news in the USA. More recently, Entman and Rojecki's *The Black Image in the White Mind* (2000) provided most welcome empirical depth in the analysis of race and the media and this will remain a key text for many years to come. A longstanding concern of mine has been the empirical emptiness of the race and media field, particularly in the UK and Europe. There is much speculation and untested theory, much anecdotal evidence but little large-scale empirical work. This book is based on an empirical project, and in the context of the literature makes no apologies for it. Despite having a concern to expose racism in the news, finding out the extent and depth of broadly anti-racist news material was surprising. We need to carefully weigh the power of continued racism and continuing anti-racism as social forces in any analysis of the operation of social institutions and this, too, is an objective of this book.

Researching this book while both in the UK during the 1997 General Election and in the USA during the 2000 Presidential Election proved invaluable. These elections showed remarkable parallels in that major protagonists all attempted not to 'play the race card', played down debates on immigration and talked-up ethnic diversity and inclusion of ethnic minorities. This relatively benign political context no doubt played a key role in influencing news coverage, yet even here strong hostile messages persisted. Whether politics and news will get any better than this in the coming century, or whether retrenching national and ethnic positions will lead to increasing media hostility in Europe and the USA is unknown. The strength of the economic and social forces which continue to drive international migration, the durability of racism over many centuries and the continued political and social divisions that are based on race and ethnicity will ensure that race remains a key news theme well into the foreseeable future.

The more recent British evidence of political and media hostility to asylum seekers documented by the European Commission Against Racism and Intolerance (www.ecri.coe.int) and reported in the UK news media (UK 'MOST RACIST' IN EUROPE ON REFUGEES, *Guardian*, 3 April 2001) substantiates the permanence of racist hostility. This setting indicates that William Hague, the leader of the Conservative Party at the time of writing, and other conservatives will continue to make connections with older political debates over the need for racialised immigration controls in the UK General Election in 2001. On 4 March in a speech at Harrogate, Hague warned that if Labour was returned to power, Britain would find itself 'heading into a foreign land'. He went on to repeatedly lay claim to backward-looking notions of Britishness and the 'natural instincts of the British people'. On 27 March John Townend, a Conservative MP, declared our 'homogenous Anglo-Saxon culture' has been undermined by massive Commonwealth immigration and new inflows of asylum seekers. These views were strongly condemned by Hague. They were, however, strongly

supported in vox pop interviews in Townend's Bridlington constitu-
ency, which accompanied coverage of his speech on the regional television news programme BBC Look North. Andrew Alexander in the
Daily Mail (6 April 2001) argues rhetorically that 'if the Tory leader
was not complaining about the arrival of large numbers whose presence was not welcome, what was he complaining about?' Whereas the
Sun's editorial (30 March 2001) declared 'Odious Rant . . Townend's
racist rant makes us despair of the Tories . . . Townend's speech was an
odious speech from an odious man'. Most recently, further exposure of
racist campaigning by Conservative Party MPs has been the subject of
numerous news items. TORY MPS REJECT ANTI-RACISM CODE
(*Guardian*, 19 April 2001), a front-page item, highlighted the failure
of three Conservative MPs to sign up to the Commission for Racial
Equality's code of conduct for the election which urges that freedom to
political expression should not be abused through the exploitation of
racism. Such events did not constitute news in the 1980s when many
Labour MPs, including left-wingers such as Eric Heffer, dismissed a
similar CRE initiative as irrelevant during General Election campaigning. These events and related coverage further illustrate two central
themes of this book. Firstly, the increasingly 'anti-racist show' put on
by white news organisations who seek to expose and ridicule racism,
and, secondly, the central role of political leadership in influencing
news coverage of race-related issues.

On 20 April 2001 the *Daily Mail* proclaimed on its front page lead
ROBIN COOK SPARKS FURIOUS ROW WITH AN ASTONISHING
DECLARATION THERE IS NO SUCH RACE AS THE BRITISH.
This followed the heightening focus on race issues in the run-up to the
UK General Election discussed above. In reply to Conservative attempts to reaffirm a backward-looking white Anglo-Saxon notion of
Britishness, Labour Foreign Secretary Robin Cook gave one of the
'strongest defences of multi-culturalism ever made by a British Minister' (*Daily Mail*). The hotly contested character of this fundamental
debate over what race is illustrates both the continuing newsworthiness
of this idea and the continuing need to clarify and carry through a
comprehensive critique of dangerous race-thinking. Roger Scruton
provides a simplistic defence of the race idea in the *Mail* stating that
British nationalism derives primarily from the 'melding' of three real
races, the English, Welsh and Scots. Should we continue to treat races
as real things, groups of people who come into contact with one
another creating nations and race relations? Support for this position

is strongly advocated in the *Mail*'s editorial comment. Fundamental issues of what constitutes a race-related issue and how the conceptualisation and measurement of racism in media representation can be carried out are addressed in the next chapter.

1

Conceptualising and Evaluating Racism in Media Representation

Introduction

Race has been a newsworthy topic of particular interest in Britain, Western Europe and the USA for over two hundred and fifty years. The news media have, over this time, been a key site for the representation of ideas about racialised groups, providing a mass of speculation, commentary and information. This cultural archive provides an immense store of knowledge, values and images that have assisted in the maintenance and reproduction of both racist and anti-racist ideas, which fuse in both historical and contemporary forms of racial ambivalence.

Fascination with the allure of race and racism and their contradictions, degradations and pleasures seem to ensure that their representation in the media, and particularly treatment and coverage in news and factual programming, remains a controversial and recurring issue of debate today. In the most recent extensive US study of race and media, including news coverage, Entman and Rojecki confirm that 'complex ambivalence' characterises white racial attitudes, and that various media, including television, film and advertising, play a 'depleting role' reducing social understanding, which shifts prevailing ambivalence towards racial animosity (2000: 44). Harmful 'voids' or silences in the media, such as the pervasive nature of white affirmative preferences in the social division of welfare, parallel the presentation of an irresponsible black social world through stereotypes of laziness, welfare cheating, murderous violence and sexual excess. This book, and the research on which it draws, develops from a similar analytical

11

concern, that of seeking to identify and address the ways in which
privileging and silencing of key themes operates in race news.

There has been remarkably little attention to pre-twentieth-century
media coverage of race, and much of the literature in this field is
concerned with contemporary analysis. However, the historical recon-
struction and writing of the history of migration and settlement of
black and minority ethnic groups frequently relied on newspapers and
other forms of news media as an important source of data, for example
in British society (Walvin, 1971; Shyllon, 1977; Lorimer, 1978).

Popular debates over slavery and abolition provided a key terrain
for the early articulation of ideas of race, and the development of
newspapers provided a mechanism for their promotion and circula-
tion. The ambivalence and violent dissension shown in these debates
was reflected in press coverage. Liverpool provides a good example of
this process. As the town grew to be Britain's top slave-trading port in
the late 1700s, and subsequently became a key site for abolition debates, the first regular local newspapers were being printed; the *Liverpool Advertiser* and the *Liverpool Chronicle* (Law, 1981). These papers
carried frequent advertisements for both slave auctions and 'handsome
rewards' for the retrieval of runaway slaves. They also contained
commentary on the value of slave-trading and justifications for the
trade which included the view that Africans liked to be 'packed into
slave ships' because they were 'treated so badly in their own country'.
This form of brutal economic racism was to be found alongside pater-
nalistic and maternalistic perspectives. A journalist's report of a slave
auction in the *Liverpool Advertiser* presents a more reflective view of
this event through the white gaze of a shopkeeper's wife:

> A young negress is pushed forward. She has the quality of a statue, scantily
> dressed. A cluster of seamen start bawdy joking among themselves, and a
> shopkeeper with his young wife on his arm draws away in disfavour. The
> woman watches the negress. She has passed through streets where slave
> collars, branding irons, thumbscrews and mouthpieces are displayed for sale.
> She knows their use but they are so remote from her experience that their
> significance has hitherto remained unreal ... but the slave girl raises fleeting
> doubts, compassion. She would like to have her as a maid servant and treat her
> well – teach her Christian values and good housekeeping. (Scobie, 1972: 18)

In this piece, the linkage of race and sexuality, the pricking of a liberal
conscience over the embarrassing issue of racism and the implied

denial of widespread popular racism are further recurrent themes to be found in both historical and contemporary news-media stories. Reading (1999: 178) also refers to this period as a time which marked the beginning of black-led strategies for news exchange and consumption as a result of exclusion, in this case from white coffee houses where newspapers were read and discussed. Members of the emerging black communities across Britain found their own places to group together to gossip and exchange information, often because they were 'liable to slights' or racial harassment (Dickens, 1861).

An explosion of sustained news coverage of issues of race and slavery appeared during the abolition debates. In the 1780s and 1790s, the general populace was bombarded with pamphlets, articles and reports in the press, street songs and poems which expressed a gamut of reasons for supporting the slave trade, as well as arguments for ending slavery. (As one London correspondent commented on the abolition issues, one was either a 'Liverpool Man' or a 'Humanity Man' (quoted in Sanderson, 1976: 225).) Many of these more alternative forms of conveying news about the abolition of slavery and racism came into use as a result of exclusion and stereotyping in the mainstream British press, eventually leading to the establishment of a vibrant black press (Reading, 1999; Benjamin, 1995). But, amongst the pro-Abolitionists such as William Roscoe, more subtle racial stereotypes were presented often idealising Africans with unintended and negative consequences. In Roscoe's words, white traders dangled baubles before the 'sons of innocence', corrupting these noble savages in the process (Roscoe, 1787, 1788). Anti-slavery sentiment was also responsible for popularising 'nigger minstrel' shows and related racist stereotypes through the Victorian period. By the 1850s, racism in Britain had both pervaded most spheres of social life and assumed a 'truth' and fixity within hierarchies of social class and status (Lorimer, 1978: 39). The subject of race provoked intellectual debate, curiosity and amusement across all classes. Racism was to be found in the scientific theories, papers and lectures of biologists, historians and anthropologists; in religious doctrines and sermons; in children's comics and books; in advertising; in entertainment through jokes and caricature; and in political debates over the morality of colonialism and Empire – all of which found expression in various media forms.

The Irish were satirised in *Punch* in 1862 as a 'creature manifestly between the gorilla and the negro . . . it talks a sort of gibberish' (Law, 1981, also see Curtis, 1971). Jewish migrants in the 1880s and 1890s

faced torrents of abuse particularly from the newly-formed mass trade
unions (Hikins, 1973). These views were regularly reported in the press
along with warnings of an 'alien flood' which provided the material stuff
of political debates over the introduction of racialised immigration
policies in the early 1900s. Chinese settlers, similarly to Jewish migrants,
faced racial hostility from national newspapers and also journals sympathetic to the cause of labour (e.g. *The Clarion* and *Justice*), with
persistent references to the 'yellow peril'. Newspaper exposés of 'Chinese vice' sought to link gambling, drug abuse and objections to sexual
relations between Chinese men and white women (Law, 1981; Clegg,
1994). Abhorrence of interracial sexual relationships has been a further
frequently repeated media message (Young, 1996: 44–8).

Blackface minstrelsy made its transition to film in 1896 in Lumiére's
The Wandering Negro Minstrels (Bourne, 1998) and continues to be a
topic of newsworthy interest. The *Daily Mail* reported on the COLLI-
SION OF RACE AND ART THAT ROCKED THE ALL-WHITE SHOW-
BOAT (26 August 1999) where Redditch Council vetoed a production
of Showboat as it involved white actors blacking-up, a practice which
has been banned by the actors' union Equity since 1995. Why this
incident warrants attention as a third of a page news story on page five
of the paper is not made clear. We are left to draw our own conclusions
as to what this item means. The tone of the article resonates with
images of 'loony-Left Councils' and 'over-the-top' anti-racism redo-
lent of 1980s news coverage. But, unlike that period, we also see
suggestions that 'blacking up' should be a thing of the past and that
in the final words of the article; 'times have changed'. References to
race seem to continually add news value to stories for many editors and
journalists although the content and meaning of the ways in which it is
represented and in which it is interpreted are fluid and dynamic.

A further historical example shows a more obvious and direct linkage
between the news media and the propagation of fascism and racism. In
the early 1930s Lord Rothermere's papers, the *Daily Mirror*, the *Sunday
Pictorial*, the *Daily Record*, the *Glasgow Evening News* and the *Sunday
Mail*, actively supported Oswald Moseley's British Union of Fascists
(Benewick, 1972; Wheeler, 1997). During this period the *Daily Mail* ran
headlines such as GIVE THE BLACKSHIRTS A HELPING HAND, and
the *Evening News* held a letter competition around the theme WHY I
LIKE THE BLACKSHIRTS (Wheeler, 1997: 44).

Racism in the media is seen as abundant and self-evident by many,
particularly black and minority ethnic consumers and campaigning

organisations such as the Coalition for Asylum and Immigration Rights and the National Assembly Against Racism. The recent 'whitewash' of network programming in the USA is a useful example (*Guardian*, 2 September 1999; Gonzalez and Rodriguez, 1999). Here, a number of national civil rights organisations, including the National Association for the Advancement of Colored Peoples and the National Council of La Raza, protested against the decision of American networks to target their autumn 1999 season of programmes at young white audiences. This led a call for a two-week television boycott of those networks under the title 'Brownout '99', because of the lack of 'brown' faces on television. In the UK, a similar challenge to major television channels was made by the Commission for Racial Equality drawing on research by Cummerbatch. This was reported in the Guardian as HIT TV SHOWS IGNORE ETHNIC MINORITIES (2 April 2001). The study found that most of the top-ten programmes in the week ending 26 November 2000, such as Eastenders, Coronation Street, Heartbeat and One Foot in the Grave, contained no ethnic minorities.

The prevalence of racism in the media is often vehemently contested or perversely ignored, and little attempt is often made to grasp the full nature and extent of racist ideas that have persisted over generations and across nations. In commenting on the wider context of racism in British society and the fact that only 3 per cent of people reported themselves as 'very prejudiced' in the British Social Attitudes Survey, Gary Younge described the 'level of pretence about racism in Britain' as 'quite staggering' (*Guardian*, 10 September 1998). Such pretence was evident in the *Daily Mail*'s defence of its inflammatory hostile coverage of migrants and asylum-seekers, where recourse was made to a formal legal position that the items were not racist. Indeed, the power of whiteness in media representation is precisely its normality and invisibility (Gabriel, 1998). In the USA, denial of anti-black discrimination was found to be the most critical element of racial animosity in a study of white attitudes in Indianapolis. This was found to accompany denial that material conditions of whites were buttressed by racial preference and privilege, and through this process produced a view that was impatient and angry about black political demands and one that saw a world where 'Blacks had somehow gotten the upper hand on Whites' (Entman and Rojecki, 2000: 43).

The complex chameleon-like character of racism, which is subject to variation and change across contexts and times, poses considerable problems for intellectual analysis. The process of conceptualisation involves constructing an adequate encompassing definition, identifying key common elements and their articulation, and operationalising these elements to enable measurement and evaluation. These issues are a focus of this chapter, which addresses wider issues in media representation other than those that relate directly to news media. Debates over racism in the media have many themes; what is racist? is treatment of issues of race, ethnicity and migration improving or becoming more hostile? whose voices are privileged and whose are silent? what social forces are driving changing patterns of news coverage, what should be done to regulate or improve such journalism, and how can prevailing news media representation of race be challenged? Three examples of attempts to engage with the conceptualisation of racism in the media in order to build a theoretical framework for responding to these types of questions are critically examined, from researchers in the Netherlands (Dijk), Australia (Jakcubowicz) and America (Shohat and Stam). Finally, a framework for evaluating racism, which is defined as the negative attribution of significations of race, in the media is developed.

Firstly, consideration is given to the problem of conceptual definition and some of the difficulties of operationalisation (Law, 1996). The notion of racism as a singular, trans-historical mode of explanation has frequently been challenged. The deflation of its explanatory power and the development of historically and culturally grounded analysis with particular attention being given to form and context are a key feature of contemporary debates. This is evident in Hall's (1992) emphasis on the 'demise of the essential black subject'. Here, the temporarily specific construction of the universal commonalities of experiencing racism amongst all black people is now giving way to exploration of the huge variety of syncretic ethnic identities which have emerged following the establishment of worldwide migrant communities (diasporas). The stuff of racism and who becomes its target varies widely within and across different nation-states. This has led to an emphasis on the specification and investigation of different racisms. But, this strategy avoids the conceptual problem of definition. Also, constructing a more robust trans-national understanding of racism is particularly important in the context of increasing global communications (Ginneken, 1998). In attempting to resolve this conceptual problem, Mason (1992), Miles (1989) and Banton (1970) all concur with the view that the use of the concept of racism should be restricted to essentially biological explanations and representations. In other words, racism refers to those situations where ideas of stock or biological difference are given social significance and symbolically mobilised (Mason, 1992: 23). The concept of racism presupposes a concept of race and is therefore to be distinguished by:

1. the signification of race characteristics to identify a collectivity;
2. the attribution of such a group with negative biological or cultural characteristics;
3. the designation of boundaries to specify inclusion and exclusion;
4. variation in form in that it may be a relatively coherent theory or a loose assembly of images and explanations;
5. its practical adequacy; in that it successfully 'makes sense' of the world for those who articulate it (Miles, 1989: 79–80);
6. its pleasures; 'an unearned easy feeling of superiority and the facile cementing of group identity on the fragile basis of arbitrary antipathy' (Shoat and Stam, 1994: 22).

The case for 'racism as fun' was recently made by Jeremy Clarkson, after being labelled a racist, in the *Independent* (CALL ME A RACIST, BUT FOREIGNERS ARE FUNNY, *Sunday Times*, 5 December 1999). Here he railed against the 'climate of intolerance' where 'you can't laugh at Johnny Foreigner'. Extending beyond individual racism, is the notion of institutional racism and here Black Power and anti-racist analysis in both the UK and the USA have been criticised for serious weaknesses evident in their use of the concept of institutional racism as an analytical tool, due to its inflation to cover the 'workings of the system' in a simplistic and undifferentiated way (Mason, 1992; Miles, 1989). The revival and redefinition of this concept in the Stephen Lawrence Inquiry is dealt with below; see *www.official-documents. co.uk/document/cm42/4262/*. This critique logically leads to a resulting deflation of the concept of racism and the rejection of its generalised application to social structures and practices (Law, 1996). This causes very real problems in policy analysis where, for example, a practice which constitutes indirect racial discrimination, as defined in the 1976 Race Relations Act, would under these formulations not generally be included as an example of racism. Legally such instances are defined as unintentional and Miles, amongst others, seeks to exclude unintentional instances from classification as racist. The problem here is that intentionality is not static and may change, as may the justification for the continuance of discriminatory practices. The argument turns on

what adequately constitutes the establishment of a 'process of determinacy' between racist discourse and its embodiment in practice. I
would support the spirit of the deflationary critique in that its intention
is to develop analytical accuracy and more effectively inform interven-
tionist strategies, but the logic in rejecting specification of policy or
institutional practices as racist where such an effect has been established over time is questionable. Firstly, a practice may have resulted
from the institutionalisation of racist discourse, which is now denied or
unsupported, yet the practice continues. In these instances the recon-
struction of 'archives' of knowledge is required to establish the racist
intent. However, in the absence of detailed evidence, or where it is
partial or fragmentary, inference of racism can easily be contested.
Secondly, when the racially discriminatory effects of particular practices become known and the practice is sustained, unintentionality
turns into intentionality and assumptions related to 'race' may come
into active operation. However, the decision to sustain a practice
which has racially discriminatory effects may be justified by 'reasonable' arguments which have no racist content. Here, equally, such
arguments may be contested as they may be felt to conceal racist
assumptions given the clear evidence that racially detrimental actions
are held to be of lesser significance. The multiple determination and
articulation of racist discourse requires specification in the same way
that the multiple determination and articulation of particular racist
policies or racist institutional practices requires detailed analysis. The
often immense difficulty of making explicit the forms and content of
racial signification operating in, say, the assumptions of an editor,
journalist, employer, or a policy-making committee, group or team,
combined with the frequency of denial in racist discourse requires
judgements to be made on the basis of available evidence. Unjustifiable
racial exclusion and procedural regulation are some of the key mechanisms in the reproduction of racial inequalities, and the quest for
'pure' racist discourse should not obscure the identification, evaluation
and questioning of such practices.

The Stephen Lawrence Inquiry has provided a new re-statement of
the meaning of institutional racism which is likely to reinvigorate
critical debate and discussion about the ways in which many organisations operate with respect to minority ethnic groups:

> Racism, institutional or otherwise, is not the prerogative of the Police
> Service. It is clear that other agencies including those dealing with housing

and education also suffer from the disease. If racism is to be eradicated there must be specific and co-ordinated action both within the agencies themselves and by society at large, particularly through the educational system, from pre-primary school upwards and onwards. (Home Office, 1999: para 6.54)

The definition of institutional racism used by the Inquiry team refers to:

The collective failure of an organisation to provide an appropriate and professional service to people because of their culture, colour or ethnic origin. It can be seen or detected in processes, attitudes and behaviour which amount to discrimination through unwitting prejudice, ignorance, thoughtlessness and racist stereotyping which disadvantage minority ethnic people. (Home Office, 1999: para 6.34)

In relation to the examination of news media, the Inquiry team's elaboration of the meaning of 'unwitting racism' is particularly relevant (1999: para 6.17). The report refers to such racism arising from both 'unfamiliarity with the cultural traditions of people and families from minority ethnic communities', and, 'racist stereotyping of black people as potential criminals or troublemakers'. These aspects are found to be common features of media racism in the analysis presented in this book.

In seeking to explain misrepresentation of ethnic minorities in the British news media, Cottle (1999) warns of the 'problem of inference', that is simply reading off racist motivation on the part of media producers from the identification of racially demeaning news items. Overcoming this problem, for Cottle, requires analysis of the process of news production, involving an investigation of both contextual factors (e.g. prevailing cultural and political discourse, market environment and journalist training) as well as determinate factors (journalist and proprietor prejudice, news values, organisation of news production and news conventions). This valuable approach echoes Miles' (1989) concern for unpicking institutional mechanisms and establishing a 'process of determinacy' between racist discourse and professional practice. Such a task is dismissed in a rather offhand fashion by Entman and Rojecki (2000: 44) who, despite their trenchant critique of race in the US media, suggest that there is no racism on the part of media producers. They 'never consciously create such imagery' we are told. They are rational people who respond to economic forces, being driven by the 'norms of objectively detached profit seeking'. Despite the use of the traditional sociological notion of a centred self which underlies this argument, where is the prevailing power of racial ambivalence which grips the US citizenry? Are television producers immune to both these contagious attitudes and the power of race-thinking embedded in language and aesthetics? Do they really *not* know what they are doing? Entman and Rojecki also confine their definition of racists purely to those who believe in classic scientific racism involving a naturalised racial order of inferiority and superiority. They prefer to elaborate a gradation of white racial attitudes outside racism, from comity (courtesy and civility towards others), through ambivalence to animosity (belief in racial stereotypes but not racial hierarchies). We would expect that this diversity of positions would be reflected, however unevenly, amongst producers of media. Indeed, they confirm that they believe most media personnel oppose blatant racism, with some vehemently opposed to it, but yet they see racial animosity being fostered in the white audience by subtle and unconscious presentation of racial difference and hierarchy (2000: 57). But should this process not also foster racial hostility amongst media personnel as well, as they do not occupy an 'above the masses' social position? There is clearly a strong similarity between this approach and use of the notion of unwitting racism in the Lawrence Inquiry. Three further conceptual frameworks which seek to develop a coherent analysis of racism in the media are examined in the next section.

Conceptualising racism: three frameworks for media analysis

Teun van Dijk provides one of the most elaborated theoretical frameworks for the analysis of racism in the media (1987, 1991, 1993). He defines racism as a 'property of ethnic group dominance', which is identified as 'the historically rooted dominance of whites (Europeans) over Others' (1993: 47). The key agents of white domination are identified as the 'elites' who 'indirectly control the minds of others' (1993: 21), for example through 'biased news reporting', and further, that racism is 'prepared' by these elites for popular consumption. Elite control of media institutions is seen as enabling control over public discourses which then 'enact, support and legitimate' white dominance

(1993: 284). There are a host of theoretical and empirical problems with this analysis including the confinement of racism to white Europeans, its necessary linkage to ethnic domination, the unitary treatment of 'whites' and the unitary treatment of elite groupings. But, in relation to the conceptual construction of racism he freely acknowledges his differentiation from the position elucidated above and proposes that racism should include discriminatory practices which are not underlain by ideas of racial superiority. Van Dijk sidesteps the problem of establishing a process of determinacy between racist ideas and actions and instead invokes a test based on the experiential knowledge of racism amongst ethnic minorities themselves. In other words, racist practices are identified when they are evaluated as such by minority group members when no other reasonable explanation can be given. Such attempts to empower and privilege the voices of minority ethnic groups have been invoked in many contexts and are implicit in recent research on black and minority ethnic audiences (Mullan, 1996; ITC, 1996; Ross, 1997). The deference to a level of essentialist experience rests on the definition of racism as being confined to whites. This is a binary model of racism, which splits the world into white and black and awards these arbitrary, mythical racial groups with exclusive and separate forms of social cognition. This is antithetical to the critique of race as a scientific and social concept. The range of genetic diversity within physiologically distinctive populations is often as wide as differences between such groups (Rose *et al.*, 1985). Equally, the spurious homogenising of social experience amongst people from a wide range of multifaceted social locations is thoroughly problematic.

There are a further range of criticisms of van Dijk's work elaborated by Ferguson (1998: 131). In particular, Ferguson is critical of the conceptualisation of both ideology and the consumption of racial stereotypes. Firstly, the implication in van Dijk's work that discourse on race is closed and shared in a society is problematic and allows little room for complexity and contradiction in both representation and consumption. Secondly, the mechanical and vague ways in which this account discusses the process whereby readers acquire ethnic stereotypes from the media is criticised. Some readers are said to be accepting news stereotypes wholesale and some to be rejecting them, we have no explanatory framework from which to assess the basis by which this is occurring. This is seen to be a speculative assertion, which appears to be based on little clear evidence.

The Racism and Media research group, at the University of Technology in Sydney, has also been concerned to develop a sustained critical analysis of these issues in the Australian context (Jakubowicz, 1994). They identify the key components of racism as being an 'intellectual/ideological framework of explanation, a negative orientation toward "the Other" and a commitment to a set of actions that put these values into practice' (1994: 27). They seek therefore to refrain from identifying practices as racist unless they clearly embody such negative orientations. This is a tighter conceptualisation of racism compared to van Dijk, and one which also requires evidence of a commitment to act. Reproduction of racism in the media is seen to be perpetuated by the conscious commitment of media practitioners to professional values embodied in, for example, recruitment practices or news production, which 'unselfconsciously integrate perceptions of racial and ethnic hierarchies' (1994: 189). Racism in this analysis cannot therefore be latent; it must be manifest through social action. The necessary identification of intention introduces key dilemmas for analysis. The denial of racist intent which characterises many contemporary forms of racist discourse, for example political discourse which advocates racialised immigration controls, would function to rule out such positions from identification as racist. The retention of an inflated construction of racism is also indicated in their account of structural racism. These instances occur where 'regular patterns of unequal access to power seems to recur, and [is] to be solely associated with race or ethnic factors' (1994: 29). The extent to which association is different from explanation or determination therefore becomes crucial to this position. There is a tendency here to use racism as an 'easy' explanation for structures of inequality that may be reproduced through a complex set of factors and processes, not least the actions of those who are the object of racism themselves. Despite these difficulties Jakubowicz and his colleagues do, however, express a similar intellectual frustration with the difficulties of establishing racist ideas underlying institutional mechanisms and practices as that outlined above.

A different approach to the analysis of racism in the media is evident in a thorough and compelling account produced by Shohat and Stam (1994). They set out an account of racism which does not seek to be universal. It is explicitly concerned with the discourse of the 'West and the Rest' (also see Hall, 1992) and what they identify as the 'discursive residue of colonialism'; contemporary Eurocentrism. Although they acknowledge that racism is not unique to the West and not solely identified with colonial situations this is their key focus. However, the significance of this acknowledgement needs to be weighed against recent evidence of the origins and strength of racist discourse outside the West. Dikotter (1997), Weiner (1997), Chow (1997) and Sato (1997) establish the independent development of racial theories and race ideas in the East, particularly China and Japan. The tendency to restrict the definition of racism to the West has worrying political implications in that it has provided a rhetorical strategy for countries in the East to resist attempts by the United Nations to promote elimination of racial discrimination (Dikotter, 1997: 2). Japan belatedly signed up to the UN Convention on racial discrimination in 1996 and subsequently events related to Japanese racism, both in Britain and in Japan itself, have begun to emerge on UK news agendas. The first successful prosecution of racial discrimination prompted the following headline, JAPAN WAKES UP TO THE PROBLEM OF RACISM (*Guardian*, 24 November 1999). Here, the target of racism in Japan has frequently been members of the Korean community, although a wider variety of migrants, or gaijin (outside people), have been subject to abuse and violence. In Hamamatsu city, the settlement of Brazilian migrants has been protested against by rightwing groups and racial discrimination is widespread, for example in private rented housing, shops and bars. The legal case involved a Brazilian woman who was refused service in a jewellery shop, which displayed the sign 'No Foreigners'. Notions of Japanese racial and ethnic purity underlie these events. In the intensive study of British news presented in Chapter 2, prosecution of racial discrimination against British employees by a Japanese firm received wide coverage.

Despite the problem of underplaying non-Western forms of racism, Shoat and Stam (1994) provide a more subtle and elaborated account of the features of racist discourse than those positions identified above, drawing particularly on psychoanalytic theory and the work of Fanon (1967). They identify racism's 'double movement of aggression and narcissism', abusing the victim and complementing the abuser, which indicates the 'pleasure' of racist expression as noted above. Ambivalence in loathing and loving the object of racism, for example in the 'seductions' of India for the colonial English, is a further theme, characterised by Hall (1992) as 'fantasies of degradation and desire'. Shohat and Stam identify six key mechanisms in the operation of their conception of 'colonial-style racism'. Projecting deficiency (in ability, civilisation etc.), establishing hierarchies, blaming the victim, coolness to claims of oppression, seeing the life of those subject to racism as of less or no worth, and the elaboration of a discourse of reverse discrimination (1994: 23–5). These mechanisms are not proposed as necessary or essential in the identification of racist discourse, but they do assist in elaborating potential aspects and dimensions of negative attribution.

Frameworks for measuring negative attribution

Bearing these difficulties in mind, it is necessary to engage with questions of operationalisation. In other words, elaborating the concept of racism so that it can be empirically measured with due regard to questions of reliability and validity. Using the definition given above, racism involves the signification of race to define a collectivity and its linkage to negative attributes. Specification is therefore required of these two key elements; the signification of race and the evaluation of negative attribution. It is crucial to stress that races are entirely mythical and imagined creations.

Our first task is to identify exactly when and where race is being referred to in a text. For example, does the use of a photograph of a person's face in a news story always carry a racial meaning? We might agree where, for example, a young, male, black offender's mugshot is used to illustrate a story of gang-rape. But we may also argue that showing white people in particular roles, for example as experts in news stories, may equally hail particular white subjectivities and convey a racial meaning. So, when is race being signified and when is it not? Further, how are we to arbitrate in disputes over racial meaning? The concept of signification draws on the analysis of signs which has developed from the work of Saussure and Barthes (see Hall, 1997b, for a thorough introduction to these ideas). A sign is the association of the signifier (a picture, word or thing) with the signified (an idea, concept, mental picture or meaning). In this case the signified, race, refers to a distinct group of persons who are seen to share common phenotypical characteristics. Signifiers of race may include words (e.g. black, white, Caucasian, Negroid, ethnic, immigrant, Gypsy) or pictures (persons of common skin colour) and are open to complexity and variation in meaning and interpretation. The invisibility or normality of constructions and representations of whiteness combined with discursive strategies of racial denial pose particular problems for media analysis (Gabriel, 1998). But, the key point that the meaning of racial representations 'can never be fixed' (Hall, 1997b: 270) is illustrated by the varied and conflicting means employed to identify and measure such meaning.

Our second task is the measurement of the negative attribution of race. This is often treated in a vague and ambiguous manner, and negative attribution may have a range of different meanings depending on how this is assessed. These include:

- measurement of negative attribution of minorities against a dominant white norm;
- assessment of racial and cultural representation in comparison to 'real' life;
- evaluation of the privileging and silencing of different cultural voices in relation to Eurocentric norms; and,
- perception of negative attribution of racialised groups by themselves.

Whitecentrism

Firstly, whitecentrism – the comparison of treatment against a 'white norm' – is often used, for example, in the assessment of the portrayal of minority ethnic groups in television programmes. Cummerbatch *et al.* (1996) analysed a sample of fictional television programmes and found that in one particular aspect of portrayal there was no negative attribution; as 6 per cent of minority ethnic characters were criminals compared to 8 per cent of white characters. This may be a useful method for the construction of arguments around issues of inequity and unfairness in programmes and films. But, this approach relies on a problematic notion of equal representation which defines difference negatively and, by implication, places a 'burden of representation' on programme makers. It implies that portrayal of minority ethnic groups should conform with the pattern of portrayal of whites, and therefore places 'white' norms at the centre of the analysis and privileges these as given and unquestioned. Problematic notions of 'less favourable treatment in comparison to the way others are normally treated' and 'disproportionate representation or exclusion in comparison to others' are found in the legal construction of the concept of racial discrimination, and their limitations have been highlighted elsewhere (Hepple and Szyszczak, 1992; Law, 1996). The 'others' in these arguments are the white ethnic majority. Here, treatment, presentation and representation use a homogenous white yardstick, which in seeking to subvert whiteness reestablishes white 'normality'. This is not to undermine the value of such 'intermediate' arguments for equity and fairness in political, organisational and managerial contexts, but to urge a deeper attention to the power of whiteness.

In the UK, work by the Glasgow Media Group (1997b, c; Philo, 1999) has also sought to operationalise whitecentric analysis through studies of the proportional representation of minority ethnic individuals as presenters and hosts on British television and in television advertising. Analysis of television programmes in June and August 1996 showed that a large section of entertainment and factual programming was exclusively 'white', for example weather forecasts, documentaries, current affairs and quiz, game and chat shows. Three programme areas stood out with high representation of minority ethnic presenters; education (19%), news (14%) and children's tv (13%). The researchers emphasised that black and Asian people tended to be in 'supporting roles and as temporary guests rather than hosts', and also that other minorities such as the Chinese are virtually absent across television. Analysis of advertising on ITV and Channel 4 in June and August 1996 was used to investigate both the presence of non-whites and the roles they occupied. Overall, it was found that there was no general underrepresentation in advertising using demographic comparison, with 5.3 per cent of non-whites in main lead roles. Some 'high-profile' areas of advertising are still all-white but this study indicates significant change. This was less evident in roles. Non-whites were found predominantly as musicians, sports persons or in exotic dress, and were less likely to appear in professional roles.

In the USA, Entman and Rojecki (2000) use this method to produce an index of media treatment of race (www.raceandmedia.com). They provide a comparison of black and white roles in film, appearance in television advertisements and entertainment shows, and representation in news stories. They are careful to distance themselves from any argument that attempts to assess quantitative representation in relation to reality; for example where reporting of black perpetrators of crime in local television and press news items may appear to be over-representation in comparison to crime statistics. However, they also seek to move beyond quantitative whitecentric analysis to unravel the discursive construction of American whiteness.

This concern to interrogate the significance and role of whiteness in media representations through a deeper analysis of meaning is a more recent feature of contemporary debates. The call to investigate whiteness and white supremacist stereotypes has been made by West (1990), Frankenberg (1993), Dyer (1997) and Gabriel (1998) amongst others. Dyer (1997: 4) refers to the need for 'the project of making whiteness strange'. In addressing methodological questions Dyer acknowledges the difficulty of this task due to the lack of an adequate 'taxonomy of typifications' which are used to represent whiteness. The process of reproduction of a range of persistently repeated images, which recur in representations of blackness in the media, was not so evident for whiteness. The huge range of representations of white people, who, Dyer says (1997: 12), are 'imaged as individual and/or endlessly diverse, complex and changing', gives rise to difficulties in selection and interpretation in media analysis. However, he identifies that whiteness can be found in 'narrative structural positions, rhetorical tropes and habits of perception' rather than in stereotypes. Here, identifying the ways in which hegemonic North European whiteness operates irrespective of the counterpositioning to non-white subjects, representations and interactions is set up as a key task. This task is carried through in the examination of representations of, for example, white heroic masculinity in films, white women in end-of-empire dramas and in photographic and film images of skin colour and aesthetics of light. Using these case studies Dyer shows the power of hegemonic whiteness in that it carries with it a symbolic sense of moral and aesthetic superiority, in other words a 'voice of authority', which he seeks to dislodge and undercut.

Gabriel (1998: 187) refers to the 'eruption of whiteness' resulting from processes of globalisation, and the reassertion of whiteness which is active in 'maintaining traditions, representing cultures and anchoring identities' in the face of rapid economic and cultural change. Interestingly, the media's role is seen here as one of the pivotal mechanisms in challenging the historically stable centrality of white dominant norms, and hence the media is cast as radically subversive in its powerful disruption of white cultural identity. Gabriel's work is particularly valuable in articulating both contemporary uses/forms of whiteness and also corresponding strategies of resistance and intervention (Table 1.1).

Elaborating whiteness provides, for Gabriel, a wider terrain for analysis of media representation than racism and also facilitates a wider

Table 1.1 Whiteness: categories and alternative strategies

Categories of whiteness	Forms of intervention
1. White pride politics: explicitly racist celebration of whiteness	1. Anti-racist politics (the politics of truth): oppositional forms of action including use of the media, public education and legal challenge which appeal to reason, objectivity and truth
2. Normative whiteness: implicitly racialised political discourses (liberal universalism and national identity) and cultural forms (sport, music, film)	2. Politics of representation: the production of diverse forms of representation which de-centre 'whiteness' and challenge essentialised representations of 'blackness' in film, tv, radio, music and art
3. Ontological whiteness: the state of 'being white'	3. Hybridising/disaggregating whiteness: contesting dominant versions of 'whiteness' e.g. through Celtic revival in Scotland, Ireland and Wales and demands for specific forms of media output
4. Progressive whiteness: a politics which condemns both white pride and normative whiteness and perpetuates 'white' dominance	
5. Subaltern whiteness: forms of 'minority whiteness' such as Irish or Jewish ethnicities	

Source: Gabriel (1998): 5–6.

discussion of interventions beyond that of anti-racist politics. This analytical approach opens up valuable terrain for discursive interrogation of media representation, which moves well-beyond the rather mechanistic strategies of assessing whitecentrism set out above. Anti-whiteness strategies are seen as encompassing issues of hybridity and diversity in media representations as well as questions of bias, accuracy and truth. Problems with privileging these latter questions are the next focus of attention.

Mimetic accuracy

Secondly, and more significantly, evaluation of negative attribution and negative representation may be made in relation to the 'real' through examination of mimetic, or imitative, accuracy. Shohat and Stam (1994) highlight the values and weaknesses of this approach, emphasising the value of a 'progressive realism' which can be used effectively to 'unmask and combat hegemonic representations'. The many examples of passionate protest over distorted representation, based on these claims for progressive realism, range from that of Pakistanis in Bradford over their portrayal as the emerging 'Muslim underclass' in a sensationalist BBC Panorama documentary, and wider criticism from Muslim groups over Islamophobia in the British media, to Native American criticism of complacent ignorance in their portrayal as Red Indians in Hollywood films. In questioning the effectiveness of this stereotypes- and-distortions approach, Shohat and Stam refer to the 'obsession with realism' which assumes that the 'real' and the 'truth' about a community are easily accessible, unproblematic and preexisting.

Eurocentrism

Thirdly, following on from this critique Shohat and Stam reject 'naive referential verism' and instead favour an analysis which focuses upon the 'orchestration of discourses and perspectives' based on a commitment to polycentric multiculturalism. This is seen as involving a move from analysing images to analysing 'voice'; where the critics' task is to pinpoint the 'cultural voices at play and those drowned out'. This involves a conceptual shift from the analysis of racism to an analysis of colonialist Eurocentrism where the basis of assessment is how far European social, economic and cultural norms are used to negatively attribute the norms of others. This Eurocentrism is defined as 'unthinking' and hence raises again the problem of intentionality. In addition, this approach clearly presupposes a consensus on the nature and form of 'European norms', ignores the extent to which these norms are the product of cultural hybridity themselves, assumes the 'others' are outside and separate to Europe, and as a result gives great latitude for interpretation and ambiguity in its implementation. This latitude is employed to excellent effect and their multidimensional nuanced analysis permits a thorough engagement with the multilayered complexity of racist discourse in the media. However, the case they establish is open to criticism precisely because others may construct different interpreted meanings and these may be at variance with their views as to the precise measurement of the extent of colonial racism and Eurocentrism in the media.

Racialised voices

Fourthly, assessment of negative attribution of race may be made through an analysis of audience perceptions of the members of that signified race. The investigation of the perceptions of black audiences in the UK as to representation on television has been carried out for BBC TV Equal Opportunities (Ross, 1997) and for the Independent Television Commission (ITC, 1996; Mullan, 1996). Ross and Sreberny-Mohammed carried out 35 focus groups with 353 viewers from black minority ethnic groups in 1995. These groups included Indians, Pakistanis, Bangladeshis, Africans and African-Caribbeans. Most viewers acknowledged progress in the more 'favourable' representation of black characters, but made a series of criticisms. These criticisms exemplify forms of assessing racism already identified; whitecentrism, a lack of realism and Eurocentrism. Privileging 'whiteness' through both a failure to portray black-on-black relationships and a strongly perceived tendency to show black characters with white partners was a key complaint. Criticism of a general lack of realism in black characterisation was made. Black characters were seen to be inhabiting a narrow range of stereotypical roles in comparison to 'realtime'. African-Caribbean viewers were critical of the representation of their communities as criminal and feckless. Eurocentrism was highlighted through criticism of a lack of cultural authenticity and attention to cultural detail in characterisation and in portrayal of domestic environments. Asian viewers were critical of the preoccupation with disasters in the developing world and with non-western cultural practices such as arranged marriage. Older Asian viewers complained of the 'over-Westernisation' of Asian characters, whereas younger Asian viewers saw this as realistic. In conclusion, Ross (1997: 244) reports both the 'aching desire for black images to be created, reported, discussed and interpreted in ways which recognise their humanity, not simply their blackness' (Daniels, 1990), and the 'unbearable scrutiny' to which black audiences subject the few black characters on television. This analysis indicates that black audiences do not have access to a separate level of essentially 'black' experience, which produces different strategies and methods of identifying and assessing racism as these are similar to those used by other critics. The key distinction, which Ross highlights, is the gulf in knowledge between 'white' media practitioners and 'black' audiences of the detail of everyday life in minority ethnic households and communities. This does privilege the role of black and minority ethnic groups as critics who have a right to be heard. The problems of counterposing these two racial categories have been identified previously and Ross is sensitive to both the homogenisation of blackness and the strategic need to retain and establish the commonalities in the perceptions of ethnic and 'racial' groups.

In 1994, the Independent Television Commission commissioned a survey of 300 Asians and African-Caribbeans over 16 to assess minority ethnic attitudes to television, which were then compared with the attitudes of a main sample of 1000 people (ITC, 1996). Interestingly, this research was also written up by Mullan (1996) who, in addition, carried out eight focus groups from a similar range of minority ethnic communities to add qualitative depth to his commentary. (The ITC's unhappiness with Mullan's anti-racist and critical commentary led to separate publishing with the ITC's own version being presented in a tighter and more concise fashion leaving more scope for reader interpretation.) The greater use of videos and the greater willingness to pay for satellite and cable amongst Asians and African-Caribbeans was identified as indicating a higher general degree of dissatisfaction with programmes available on terrestrial television (ITC, 1996: 16). In summing up their views, only 35 per cent of African-Caribbeans felt that the four main channels gave them all the viewing choices they wanted, compared to 56 per cent of Asians and 71 per cent of the main sample. Mullan, however, goes on to identify that this dissatisfaction stems from the perceived dominance of whitecentric and Eurocentric programme content. Eighty-eight per cent of African-Caribbeans and 76 per cent of Asians felt that all too often television generally portrayed negative stereotypes of minorities, compared to 52 per cent of the main sample.

Minority ethnic perceptions of news programmes were a key focus of these reports. Television was generally seen as the most trusted source of international, national and local news, but minority ethnic groups had less trust than the majority and more trust in radio.

Table 1.2 Impartiality of news and current-affairs programmes on the
four main broadcast channels in relation to ethnic minorities

	African-Caribbeans (%)	Asians (%)	Main sample (%)
Anti ethnic minorities	59	37	12
Fair	12	51	71
Pro ethnic minorities	19	11	13
Unweighted base size (nos.)	153	164	1452

Source: ITC, *Television: Ethnic Minorities' Views* (1996): 37.

Television was, however, generally felt to be the source of the most fair
and unbiased national news for 70 per cent of the main sample, 54 per
cent of Asians and 51 per cent of African-Caribbeans. Radio was in
second place with 12 per cent, 13 per cent and 20 per cent respectively
and the press last with 7 per cent, 13 per cent and 9 per cent respectively. In general, the main sample of viewers felt that news and current-
affairs programmes were fair (71%) towards minority ethnic groups,
with slightly more bias in favour of these groups (13%) than against
(12%). Whereas 59 per cent of African- Caribbeans and 37 per cent of
Asians saw these programmes as biased against them through perpetuation of stereotypes, lack of explanatory context and choice of issues
for inclusion and exclusion, as Table 1.2 shows.

Minority ethnic viewers in this research readily identified offensive
racism on television, but just under a half of Asian and African-
Caribbean viewers found nothing at all offensive on television.
About one in six (17%) African-Caribbean viewers identified racism
on BBC1, BBC2, ITV and Channel 4 as the prime cause of offence.
Asian viewers were more likely to be offended by sex, violence and bad
language, with one in 12 (8%) being offended by racism. This compared to 5 per cent of the main sample.

Assessment of the negative attribution of racial categories in the
media is subject to significant variation across ethnic groups. This
indicates the ethnic stratification of meaning 'decoded' from media
items. Such stratification is also evident, and to be expected given the
differentiation in forms of racist discourse, in the perception of different racial categories. In a different book Mullan (1997) draws on
Broadcasting Standards Council (BSC) research into viewers' attitudes, which is seen to be comparable to many of the findings of the

Table 1.3 Acceptability of racist terms of abuse

| Racist term of abuse | Acceptability | | | |
	Not at all (%)	Not very (%)	Fairly (%)	Very (%)
Nigger	55	27	40	4
Wog	49	29	17	5
Coon	44	32	20	4
Paki	40	29	24	6
Wop	40	28	25	7
Yid	39	30	24	7
Darkie	39	30	24	7
Dago	34	30	31	5
Chink	32	32	29	7
Honky	27	33	32	8
Nip	30	27	35	8
Kraut	22	28	40	10
Frog	21	25	42	12
Jap	20	25	43	11
Mick	11	19	50	19
Taffy	11	15	52	21
Paddy	11	15	51	22
Jock	10	14	54	22

Sources: Mullan (1997): 127; data repercentaged to exclude those who had not heard of the term or did not reply, and taken from BSC *1991 Annual Survey*, Research International.

ITC survey. This gave data on the varying acceptability of specific terms of racist abuse (see Table 1.3).

The first column of Table 1.3 shows that anti-black terms of abuse such as nigger were least acceptable, whereas much less offence was given by the use of anti-white forms of racist abuse such as Honky, Mick, Paddy, Taffy and Jock. This finding would indicate greater sensitivity to and opposition to anti-black racism on the part of over half of the viewers of British television. In contrast, Mullan emphasises the data in the third column which shows the 'alarming' finding that for significant numbers of viewers many of the terms of racial abuse were fairly acceptable; for example Paddy (51%), Nigger (40%), Kraut (40%) and Dago (31%).

Despite these findings, criticism of perceived bias and sources of offence by viewers was accompanied by support for inclusive programming. Sixty-three per cent of the main sample felt that ethnic minority issues should be part of regular television news, and over 70 per cent felt that television should cater for all ethnic communities and had a responsibility to allow access to minority ethnic groups. These findings clearly indicate the ambivalence in viewers' attitudes and, for some, the ability to simultaneously support racist abuse, multiculturalism and racial inclusion.

Conclusion

The assessment of the extent of racism in media representation is likely to be highly variable dependent on topic, theme, content and context, as well as the racial and ethnic identity of the viewer. In this sense it is necessary to disaggregate the analysis of producer intentions, textual and visual content and viewer/listener/reader reception. Nevertheless, the methods of evaluating negative attribution in media content – whitecentrism, a lack of realism and Eurocentrism – are particularly common to those who are members of racialised groups and these approaches will inform the examination of news coverage later in this study. This study is concerned primarily with news content and it is proposed that racism – or more specifically its key components, racial signification and negative attribution – can be identified and evaluated irrespective of questions of *intention* on the part of writers, producers, editors and journalists, or *reception* by listeners, viewers and readers. This does not undermine the significance and importance of seeking to understand and reveal these connections, but, as Shohat and Stam argue in relation to studying cinema:

> No deconstructionist fervour should induce us to surrender the right to find films [or news] sociologically false or ideologically pernicious, as objectively racist. (1994: 178)

To develop this position a little further; there is no necessary correspondence between racist attitudes, ideas and intentions, on the part of news producers, and racist news items. Well-intentioned media producers may produce storylines which are read as deliberately hostile and insulting to particular minority groups, or which are seen as imbued with whitecentric norms and judgements, or which are heard as drowning out the words and opinions of minority individuals. This contention is explored in Chapter 3 using the example of representation of young blacks involved in gang-rape. Similarly it is argued that there is no necessary correspondence between racist news items and audience racism; racist messages may or may not, therefore, be appropriated or even recognised by the consumer. So, some, particularly white news consumers, may be totally oblivious to the forms of racism encapsulated in a news item, others may appropriate a racist message and convert it into part of their everyday world, while others may recognise such items and reject the message. This variation in patterns of audience reception, and in producer intentions, does not undermine the importance and significance of the task of analysing, identifying and challenging the way in which racialised individuals and groups are constructed in the news. The purpose of Chapter 2 is primarily concerned to address this analytical task in relation to news on British television and radio, and in the national and regional press.

2

British News : The 'Great Anti-Racist Show'?

Introduction: the death of racism or a case to answer?

In a recent account of the sociology of journalism, Brian McNair claims that 'racism is dying' and that racists are 'increasingly isolated, finding no endorsement of their views from the media' (1998: 31). As this chapter will show, McNair is tragically wrong. The extent to which news media continue to shape the process of racialisation in a variety of terrains, particularly those of crime, social pathology, migration and both normative and progressive whiteness requires careful scrutiny. The capacity for renewal of hostile news messages about groups who are positioned outside the white nation by news producers is regularly demonstrated year after year. Running alongside this significant core of racial hostility and migrant animosity is a parallel set of news stories which counterpose and document an undeniable message of social inclusion, opposition to racism and a vision of racial justice. The nature, scope and extent of these opposing news themes is the focus of this and subsequent chapters.

Studies of the news across the UK, USA, Canada, Netherlands, Germany, France, Italy and Australia have all produced findings that show the complex ways in which ideas about 'race' have been reproduced through reporting about minority ethnic groups and migration (Jakubowicz, 1994; van Dijk, 1991; Campbell, 1995; Valdiva, 1995; Iyengar and Reeves, 1997; Meyers, 1997). A common finding has been the confinement of coverage to a set of limited topics (van Dijk 1993):

- *Immigration* and associated debates over numbers, illegal entry, fraudulent activities, forms of confinement and control, and the threat to society, culture and nation.

- *Crime* with special attention given to racialised crime such as mugging, rioting, drugs offences, prostitution and violent offences.
- *Cultural difference*, which is often inflated, negatively interpreted and linked to social problems, including inner city decline and unemployment.
- *Ethnic relations*, including inter-ethnic tension, violence and discrimination.

In addition, the silence on a range of topics of relevance to ethnic minorities, the prominence given to white news actors, and the marginalisation of minority representatives, minority women and anti-racist voices have been subject to criticism. Analysis of selected sources from the British press in the 1980s showed that in only 3.8 per cent of items on minority ethnic affairs were groups allowed to speak for themselves (van Dijk, 1993: 254).

The form and content of racism in British society is continually subject to remaking and transformation partly through news coverage. These representations of race have included the brutal and pragmatic economic racism of the slave trade era, the paternal and idealised imagery of the noble savage, the caricatures of minstrelsy, the Victorian science of racial inferiority and the vilification of intermarriage, 'half-castes' and emerging poor black communities in British cities in the 1920s and 1930s (Lorimer, 1978; Law, 1981). Cottle's (1992, 1999) review of the relevant literature has also identified that in the 1950s and 1960s Asian and African-Caribbean migrants were cast as a 'numbers' problem linked to urban decline, public ill-health and violence and disorder. In the 1970s, the period of the 'Great Moving-Right Show' in British politics, immigrant numbers, young black muggers and the conflict between the extreme Right and anti-racist organisations were dominant news themes (Hall *et al.*, 1978).

Gordon and Rosenberg (1989) used selected examples and van Dijk (1991) a more exhaustive content and discourse analysis to substantiate a comprehensive critique of racism in the British press in the 1980s. In addition, the Runnymede Trust produced, and still produces, regular monthly press watch items in their *Bulletin* which seek to document race coverage. The key problems that have been identified are the variety of ways in which black and Asian people have been portrayed as a threat to white British society, particularly through treatment of immigration and law and order themes in a range of problematic ways as shown in Box 2.1.

Box 2.1   Summary of criticisms of racism in the British press, 1980–95

Dominance of racial categorisation

● Racial categories predominate, 'ethnic' references rarely used, immi-grant much less frequent, specific nationality references rare (1985/6 data, van Dijk 1991:55).

Letting racist views dictate the news agenda

● Extensive publicity given to Enoch Powell as an expert on race relations which created a climate of racist public opinion portraying the country as under threat from black immigration (1968–88).

● Endorsed statements of 'new racism' by politicians (Gordon and Klug, 1986).

Racialising the immigration debate

● The reporting of Tamil refugees to the UK in 1985 framed these as an immigrant flood threatening the country i.e. the *Mail*, the *Sun*, the *Express* and the *Telegraph*. The *Guardian*, *Today*, the *Observer* and the *Morning Star* criticised government policy. The conclusion drawn is that 'the overall impression from the national papers was that if the government did not act quickly, the country would be swamped by a tide of bogus refugees' (Gordon and Rosenberg, 1989: 7).

● Inflation of reporting about illegal immigration through visitors visas from the African and Indian sub-continent (1986).

● Presenting refugees and asylum-seekers as a threat (RT *Bulletin*, Nov. 1992), a further analysis of the *Sun*, *Telegraph* and *Mail* during September–December 1995 showed continued characterisation of migrants and asylum-seekers as a 'flood, wave or tide', as a 'bogus' group who were defrauding the state and the taxpayer (RT *Bulletin*, Jan. 1996), little voice was given to migrant and refugee groups or the views of individuals themselves, and their was rare reporting of human-rights abuses driving asylum-seeking.

Attacks on cultural difference

● Treatment of marriages for immigration convenience e.g. the *Mail*'s Brides for Sale story, were inaccurate, unsupported, attacked ar-ranged marriage, reinforced stereotypes of Asian culture and built support for racialised immigration controls (1985).

● Definition of Islam and Muslims as a threat (1989 Rushdie Affair, 1990s Islamophobia report).

Box 2.1 cont.

Criminalising minorities

• Black and Asian migrants pictured as welfare scroungers, enjoying luxuries at the taxpayers expense by the *Mail*, *The Times*, the *Express*, the *News of the World*, the *Sun* (1986).
• Black people portrayed as a law-and-order problem through reporting of black crime statistics (1982), Black Peoples' Day of Action (1981), riots (1981–86), in particular defining looters or murderers prominently but irrelevantly as 'black' in the headlines.

Editorial shaping of racial hostility

• Use of editorial and opinion columns to reinforce racist analysis, myths, stereotypes and undermine anti-racism, through attention to a number of themes; need for racialised immigration control, multiracial society seen as a threat to British national culture, opposing anti-discrimination and anti-racist methods and motives and stereotyping black and Asian culture.
• Explicit racist messages in cartoons.
• Black sporting stories used to reproduce racist stereotype that blacks innately good at sport.

Silence on minority issues

• Press silence on black people as victims of violence (UK *Press Gazette*, 6 June 1994), the tabloids heavily dramatise and negatively portray minority ethnic news events, with the exception of racial attacks which are seen as being correctly defined as forms of 'terror'.
• Silence on analysis of issues from within minority communities and representing the range of perspectives they encompass (Gordon and Rosenberg, 1989: 34), 'perspective of ethnic groups systematically discredited' (Dijk, 1991: 69), little coverage of housing, work and health (van Dijk, 1991: 82), academic research virtually ignored, little coverage of discrimination generally.
• Minority women and representatives of minority organisations invisible as news actors (van Dijk, 1991: 85), whereas white groups play a dominant role.
• *Mail* and *Express* support for victims of immigration control rare and selective, support for the Pereira family campaign (1984) was seen as an exception that involved no questioning of immigration laws.

Box 2.1 cont.

Denial of racism

- Semantic strategies to deny, conceal, mitigate or excuse racism, blame victims and accuse anti-racists (van Dijk, 1991: 198).
- Using Asian 'millionaire' and business success stories to deny racism in Britain.

Attacks on anti-racism

- Stylistic and rhetorical strategies used to vilify blacks and anti-racists, i.e. lexical abuse.
- Undermining anti-racism through attacks on race relations law and the CRE, local authority anti-racism (Brent's 'race spies', Dewsbury dispute, Burnage report, Honeyford dispute), and denying racism and racial discrimination.

Comparing analysis of headline coverage in 1985/86 to 1989, van Dijk notes that 'ethnic reporting has become less negative and aggressive', and also that 'further research is necessary to determine whether this is a manifestation of a more general tendency to subtlety in race reporting in the UK' (1991: 58). A reduction in the number of ethnic/race items was also identified with an average of 33 items per week in *The Times*, the *Telegraph*, *Mail*, *Sun* and *Guardian* in 1989 compared to 104 per week in 1985. Coverage is described as deteriorating to an 'affair' or 'scandal' approach over this period. Overall, coverage is seen as less blatantly racist than in the 1960s and 1970s but that stereotypes and definitions of minorities as a 'problem' and 'threat' are still a persistent problem (van Dijk, 1991: 245).

Analysis of national press coverage of racial harassment and racial violence in relation to the Peter Thurston case in 1995 by the Runnymede Trust confirmed that improvement had occurred. It found that reporting by the *Daily Star* and *Today* showed greater awareness and sensitivity. But, at worst, denial of racism and racial injustice and, at best, discomfort with handling racism issues remained a problem (*Bulletin*, October 1995).

Statham's (1999) analysis of the *Guardian* from 1990–96 shows the overwhelming dominance of pro-minority/anti-racist ideologies in 1300 'claims-making acts' in the migration and ethnic relations field which were reported. The support for the Stephen Lawrence Campaign by the *Daily Mail* with a clear commitment to using press power in the pursuit of racial justice, which occurred during the data-collection period of the study reported on in this chapter, is a further indicator of change. The extent of changes in bias and quantity of coverage, together with assessment of changes in the problem areas identified above will be considered below.

There is a long tradition of critical analysis of the representation of black minorities on British television (Hartmann and Husband, 1974; Critcher *et al.*, 1975; Hall *et al.*, 1978; Hall, 1995; Holland, 1981; Tumber, 1982; Murdock, 1984; Barry, 1988; Twitchin, 1988; Daniels and Gerson, 1989; Pines, 1992; Ross, 1992, 1996; Gillespie, 1995; Mullan, 1996; Cottle, 1992, 1997):

> As a matter of routine, Britain's black and ethnic minorities have tended to be depicted in terms of a restricted repertoire of representations character-ised by conflict, controversy and deviance. (Cottle, 1996: 3)

Apart from negative portrayal, absence has been equally criticised:

> It is the poverty of black images rather than the frequency that is the real problem, images constrained and constructed within a narrow band of character types in comedy and drama, or fetishized within a racialized demonology in factual programming. (Ross, 1996: 170)

This has implications for those concerned to challenge prevailing forms of representation:

> It is the paucity of black images, outside of race-relations narratives, which are clearly about some aspect of the black 'condition' which causes those few which are screened to bear the unacceptable burden of representing all. (Ross, 1996: 177)

Nevertheless, television is a rapidly changing medium and it is import-ant to acknowledge progress that has been achieved:

> There is no denying the much greater visibility, the wider access, of black practitioners, black representations and black culture on British televi-sion...[but breakthroughs are] much more fitful and marginal in serious documentary and current affairs. (Hall, 1995: 14)

A study of regional television news showed that 'differences in news form and programme ambitions occasionally allow for a more "posi-tive" and multi-culturalist orientation to both news subject matter and audience' (Cottle, 1997: 3). The importance of television news for ethnic minorities was stressed in a different way by Gillespie, who, in her study of television consumption by young Asians in Southall found that television news was the programme type most often watched with the family and talked about with parents:

> Participation in the domestic ritual of news viewing is perceived to function as a kind of 'rite of passage' both to adult status and to effective British citizenship particularly when young people are called upon to act as translators and interpreters of the national news agenda. (1995: 101)

Young people also found news difficult to understand, uninteresting and unenjoyable. Nevertheless, 'news talk' was a key cite for the construction, negotiation and 'mix and fix' of collective identities, involving the ability to locate oneself across a multitude of social categories and frames of reference.

In comparison to the above there has been relatively little research on the treatment of race on radio. A study of journalists working in radio, as well as the press and television, identified the very low level (about 2 per cent) of black, Asian or Arab staff, and also that 19 per cent of all staff had personal knowledge and experience of ethnic prejudice in the newsroom (Delano and Henningham 1995, also see Ainley 1995). As regards listeners, black and minority ethnic people are twice as likely to listen to commercial or independent radio stations than the BBC (BBC Broadcasting Research, 1996) which may indicate neglect of such listeners and their needs (*Bulletin*, March 1996).

News journalism has been described as 'one of the key social and cultural forces in our society' (McNair, 1995: 14). In this context, evidence of racial stereotypes in news coverage is particularly worrying. Previous research has established a strong case to answer, although to date this research has failed to assess the 'big picture' of overall news coverage and has frequently been piecemeal and selective. There is also recognition that change is underway, however 'fitful and marginal' that might be.

In contrast to a focus on the range of problems the media faces in producing news in a multiracial context, its value has also been highlighted. The importance of news media as 'advocates for victims of oppression' has been stressed, particularly through the 'large stock of anti-authority frames' available 'for those antagonists who have the resources and skills to use them' (Wolfsfeld, 1997: 5). In addition, the inability of the government to restrict access to the widely varying range of news sources in relation to race and racism in the UK gives greater independence to the news media. In this context, we might expect to see a range of differing positions and voices in news coverage rather than the opposite. The influence of elites in setting media frames on race also depends on the extent of consensus. The strength of the condemnation of racism across elites in the UK, particularly in public contexts, would lead us to expect that this would have a key influence on news journalism.

Race in the British news: a case study

The *Observer* proudly, and rather optimistically, proclaimed GOODBYE XENOPHOBIA on its front page on 4 May 1997 after the Labour election landslide victory. The extent to which we have said goodbye to racism and xenophobia in news coverage across the media is itself the object of this case study. There have been longstanding concerns over the treatment of issues of race, ethnicity and migration by politicians and subsequent reporting in the British news media, but little research has focused on differing patterns of coverage across radio, television and the press. This study seeks to fill this gap through a systematic content analysis of news output from press, radio and television sources over a six-month period from November 1996 to May 1997. This analysis therefore provides a thorough contextual analysis of race and news coverage of the General Election. (For the report of this study see Law with Svennevig and Morrison, 1997, and Law, 1997a.)

This case study is concerned to provide a careful and constructive analysis of changing patterns of news coverage which is sensitive to the contested and often polarised nature of debates over race and the media. One focus of attention, particularly during General Election campaigns, has been the 'playing of the race card' by political leaders, candidates or campaigners through the media, and this is examined as part of this study. But, concern over this issue has often obscured the lack of debate over the real issues of addressing race and ethnicity in a range of public policy fields, including the media. This study therefore seeks to identify not only those race debates which are privileged in news agendas, but the silences as well.

The study centres on analysis of selected media output; a strategy which was adopted for two reasons. Firstly, the numbers of press, television and radio outlets available in the UK are large and would require research resources beyond the scope of this project. Secondly, it is assumed that race-related issues which are of genuine political significance will enter the media at a relatively 'high' mass level (i.e. national media or main regional media).

The sample of media sources (Table 2.1) was determined by consideration of which news media attract significant audiences/readerships and/or which have an established opinion-leading role. Media sources chosen consist of five TV channels (including Sky News, available to around 20 per cent of the population), four broadsheets and three tabloids (and their Sunday equivalents), two regional newspapers and three national BBC radio stations and the syndicated news service which supplies most of the ILR radio services (INR). Problems in

Table 2.1 Media output selected for analysis

National *TV*		Main evening news programmes on BBC 1
		(9 O'clock news and Saturday/Sunday equivalents)
		Main evening news programmes on BBC 1
		(9 O'clock news and Saturday/Sunday equivalents)
		Main evening news programmes on ITV
		(News at Ten and Saturday/Sunday equivalents)
		Main evening news programmes on Channel 4
		(7 O'clock news and Saturday/Sunday equivalents)
		Newsnight on BBC 2 (Monday to Friday)
		Sky News (8pm-9pm each day)
	Radio	BBC Radio 1 News headlines – (early morning)
		BBC Radio 4 Today (6.30a.m.–9a.m.
		Monday to Friday)
		BBC Radio 5 news bulletins
		INR news bulletins (8a.m.)
	Press	*The Times, Sunday Times*
		Guardian, Observer
		Daily Telegraph, Sunday Telegraph
		Independent, Independent on Sunday
		Daily Mail, Mail on Sunday
		Sun, News of the World
		Mirror, People
Regional *Press*		*London Evening Standard* and the
		Yorkshire Evening Post

data collection from INR sources have led to only a small number of items being identified. Two regional newspapers were selected which covered areas with relatively large and relatively small minority ethnic populations (Greater London and Yorkshire and Humberside which respectively have 22.2 per cent and 4.6 per cent minority ethnic populations; OPCS, 1994).

The output was collected through videotaping all TV coverage, purchase of relevant papers and audio-taping radio programmes. These were then scanned for any relevant coverage and items/stories were marked for subsequent content analysis. In the identification of items the key criterion was that items should contain reference to race or ethnicity and be related to UK debates. News about Irish terrorism was excluded as this has been covered extensively elsewhere (McNair, 1996), and also news of the many international ethnic conflicts that did not pertain directly to the UK were excluded. Wolfsfeld's (1997) book on news coverage of the Palestinian intifada and the Gulf War provides a valuable analysis of such journalism emphasising in particular the dynamic connections between politics and the news. This theme is examined here particularly in relation to questions of migration. Formal content analysis of specified items of output was then carried out with regular reliability checks on coding decisions. Data was input, verified and analysed using SPSS for Windows.

A pilot study of media output during the Party Conference 'season' (23 September to 13 October 1996) was carried out to test research instruments and data collation systems. The pilot led to a number of changes in data collection and coding and results are therefore not included with the main data set. The main data set covers the period Monday 18 November 1996 to Sunday 11 May 1997, excluding the Christmas and New Year period of 23 December 1996 to 5 January 1997. Over the 23 weeks of the study a total of 1295 items were identified, with on average 56 items appearing per week. But, there was significant variation across this period as might be expected. There was a peak of about 100 items per week during mid-February and a low of about 35 items per week from mid-March to early April. There is evidence of some decline in coverage since the 1980s. The average of 27 items per week in *The Times*, the *Telegraph*, *Guardian*, *Mail* and *Sun* in this study compares to 33 per week in 1989, and 104 per week in 1986.

A small number of key events triggered high points in media coverage, which included the following:

- criticism of the employment of Finnish nurses in a London hospital with a significant black clientele by Diane Abbott, a black British MP (November 1996);
- John Major's trip to India and his related bid to woo the Asian vote (January 1997);
- verdict of 'unlawful killing in a racially motivated attack' by the inquest into Stephen Lawrence's death (February 1997);
- debates over the playing of the 'race card' in the General Election campaign (March 1997); and
- the racially motivated rape of an Austrian tourist in London (April 1997).

As regards distribution across different media; 74 per cent of items were found in the press (of which 34 per cent were tabloid items and 66 per cent broadsheet items), 14 per cent on television and 12 per cent on radio. The main media sources in each category were the *Daily Mail* (44 per cent of tabloid items), the *Guardian* (29 per cent of broadsheet items), Radio 4 (74 per cent of radio items) and BBC 1 (28 per cent of television items).

Themes and messages: the dominance of anti-racist news

News coverage of race issues in Britain is dominated by stories which are in a variety of ways opposed to racism. This represents a dramatic change, particularly in press coverage since the 1980s. However, the bulk of previous research has ignored or underplayed this 'big picture', focusing instead on problematic issues. The purpose of this chapter is to present an analysis of the main themes and messages contained in the 1295 separate news items identified in this study. A large number of headlines are given to illustrate these themes and messages. Thematic category has been analysed in three ways. Firstly, the main broad theme that describes the content of each item such as crime, work or immigration was identified. Secondly, items were grouped into categories that described their key message about minority ethnic groups and racism; for example pro-immigrant or anti-immigrant. Thirdly, a much more detailed analysis of about 190 discursive categories was developed that enables a more precise identification of specific sub-themes.

Race-news themes

In terms of thematic content, the top two categories encompassed items relating to aspects of crime (16 per cent), closely followed by items about work (15 per cent), particularly racial-discrimination stories. The General Election and aspects of race were discussed in about 14 per cent of items and items about asylum-seekers accounted for 11 per cent. Secondary thematic categories each contained about 4–6 per cent of items overall, which included sport, immigration, racist attitudes, social welfare issues and the extreme right. Thirdly, a cluster of other categories contained 3 per cent or less items including education, entertainment, multi-culturalism, Jews, Islam/Muslims, Britishness, anti-racism/racial-equality issues, riots, Scottish/Celts and historical stories.

The primary theme was that encompassing news which linked race and crime in a variety of conflicting ways. The regular output of items which link race, violence, dangerousness and crime raises worrying questions over the unnecessary use of race references and the extent to which racialised views are being reproduced. For example, NEW WARNING AFTER RAPE BY BOGUS MINICAB DRIVER (*Daily Telegraph*, 26 November 1996) and a number of items about an Asian police constable who 'demanded sex from prostitutes' (*Daily Telegraph* and *The Times*, 11 January 1997) used irrelevant references to Asian identity. In contrast, there are a number of items which appropriately link references of race to crime, most significantly in the case of the rape of an Austrian tourist where a racial motivation was alleged, GANG RAPE OF WHITE TOURIST WAS RACIST: QC (*Sun*, 10 April 1997). But, anti-racist reporting was also evident within this racialised context. During the two-week period of 3–16 February, crime items jumped dramatically to 48 per cent of total race coverage due particularly to the Stephen Lawrence case. The tone of this coverage was generally favourable to the plight of the Lawrence family, most notably the *Daily Mail* front page, MURDERERS 14 February 1997, which commented on the 'damage to race relations' of the Lawrence case. This front page was preceded by WHITE JUSTICE FAILED MY SON (*Daily Mail*, 11 February 1997). The use of the media to raise issues of racial injustice has been a regular theme in news coverage and the *Daily Mail* has in the past taken a similar type of stance (see Chapter 1). Criticism of the white youths in question and of the criminal justice system was marked, together with positive treatment

Table 2.2   Themes by media type (%)

Theme	Tabloids	Broadsheets	Radio	Television
Crime	19	13	20	20
Work	18	16	9	12
Gen. Election	11	15	6	21
Asylum-seekers	8	8	22	13
Immigration	7	4	6	7
Sport	10	5	3	5
Racist attitudes	5	5	5	3
Social welfare	3	5	5	3
Extreme right	3	4	5	3
Entertainment	3	5	4	0
Education	3	4	1	1
Multiculturalism	1	3	4	1
Jews/Gypsies	2	3	2	3
Racial equality	1	3	1	5
Muslims/Islam	1	3	0.5	0
Britishness	2	1	3	0.7
Riots	1	1	4	0
Scottish	0.3	0.9	0.5	0.7
Other	1.7	1.1	0	1.6
Total	100	100	100	100

of the quest for racial justice; for example, FAMILY'S FRUITLESS
FIGHT FOR JUSTICE (*Guardian*, 14 February 1997), BRITAIN ALLOWS
RACE MURDERS (*Daily Telegraph*, 11 February 1997), MURDERED
BLACK TEENAGER UNLAWFULLY KILLED (Sky News, 13 February
1997).

Clear differences were evident across the media as to the attention
given to each theme as set out in Table 2.2. To summarise the variation
in thematic emphasis across different media sources an analysis of
Table 2.2 is now given. The tabloids gave more attention, relative to
other media sources, to items concerning:

- *work* items which primarily dealt with racial discrimination in
  employment;
- *sport*, particularly accusations of racism and black sporting
  achievements; and
- *immigration*, but the proportion of 'race' coverage devoted to this
  was similar to TV.

The tabloids gave equal attention to items covering crime and racist attitudes, but less attention to items covering General Election and race, asylum seekers, social welfare and the extreme right. When examining the dominant theme in race news – that is, crime – it is interesting to note that the tabloids are not primarily responsible for persisting in reproducing this set of discurive linkages. More crime items in terms of numbers were printed in the broadsheets (80 compared to 60 in the tabloids), and radio and television had a higher percentage of crime items amongst those concerned with aspects of race in the UK. Also, there are a preponderance of items concerned with exposing racism and racial discrimination and highlighting black achievements. This will be examined further below.

The broadsheets gave greater attention to items concerning work, the General Election, entertainment, anti-racism and racial equality and Islam/Muslims. They gave equal attention to racist attitudes items, and less attention to crime, asylum-seekers, immigration, Britishness and riots.

Radio gave greater attention to items concerning crime, asylum-seekers, extreme right, multiculturalism, Britishness and riots. Comparatively less attention was given to work, General Election, sport, education, racial equality and Muslim issues.

Television gave greater attention to crime, General Election, immigration and anti-racism/racial equality issues. Comparatively less attention was given to racist attitudes, social welfare, extreme right, entertainment, education and multiculturalism. Racism in sport, Muslim issues and Britishness did not make the television news during this period.

Overall, these different news media chose to select and emphasise different race-related stories which reflect underlying editorial agendas and news values. Black people are predominantly presented as criminals, victims of racism and problematised migrants. In contrast we see, for example, a very limited engagement with debates about the nature of Britishness and multiculturalism which changed in October 2000 with the controversy over the Runnymede Trust report on the Future of Multi-Ethnic Britain (*Guardian* Editor, 13 October 2000).

Race-news messages

About three-quarters of items can be identified as broadly presenting an anti-racist message. News coverage is, then, dominated by a broadly anti-racist agenda. Anti-racism has been defined rather narrowly in the British context (Law, 1996), particularly through its linkage to municipal anti-racism in the 1980s. The term is used here in a wider sense to refer to media frames (Wolfsfeld, 1997) which seek to expose and criticise racist attitudes, statements, actions and policies, which address the concerns of immigrant and minority ethnic groups and show their contribution to British society, and which embrace an inclusive view of multicultural British identity.

In contrast to the abundance of articles exposing racism and racial discrimination of various sorts there were relatively few items that carried 'denial discourse' as their main message. The argument that denial of racism is a key element of modern, newer forms of racism is not contradicted by this finding. Indeed, claims that what is being said is not racist are indicative of the influence of broadly anti-racist perspectives, and such expression can be found in many forms of racism that still persist in the news, particularly in the discussion of migration. Recent evidence from the USA confirms the significance of denial in white public opinion where black disadvantage is predominantly seen as arising from a lack of individual motivation, and the existence of continuing racial discrimination is rejected (Entman and Rojecki, 2000: 47). Such racism would have been contradicted by the evidence from analysis of US network news programmes as the authors also found a significant numbers of news items here that dealt with racial discrimination of various types. But this, they argue, also contributes to white racism, as highlighting black victims of discrimination, together with black criminality, facilitates the presentation of 'a face of Black disruption' in the news (2000: 209). This apparent contradiction is resolved through understanding the irrational, synthetic nature of white racism and its organic ambivalence as it can fuse both ideas in the discourse of victim-blaming and individual responsibility. Here, black people are seen as responsible for their failure to achieve social and economic equality. The invisibility of the pervasive character of white racial preferences and privileges in news material, a key silence, promotes such thinking. In the UK, however, there is a much greater mass of material and evidence concerning white racism and white racial discrimination in the news in comparison to the USA. The denial of continuing discrimination in society is therefore much harder to sustain, and this should play a key role in the formation of white attitudes, particularly through the tendency to remember repeated media messages. Table 2.3 presents

Table 2.3   Key messages in race and news coverage

Message	%(no.)	Message	%(no.)
Anti-immigrant	6.3 (81)	Pro-immigrant	9.3 (121)
General Election anti-minorities	2.6 (34)	General Election pro-minorities	14.1 (182)
Minorities as a social problem	11.1 (144)	Minority contributions to society	4.5 (58)
Denying racism	2.1 (27)	Exposing racism	37.6 (487)
Anti-multicultural UK	0.9 (12)	Pro-multicultural UK	2.9 (37)
Restricting opportunities	0.5 (7)	Improving opportunities	5.6 (72)
Sub-total	23.6 (305)		74 (957)
Other	6.4 (85)		
Total	100 (1295)		

an analysis of news items in relation to their key discursive messages. Clearly the meaning constructed by any item is not fixed and each may be read in a variety of ways, but here we are more concerned with linguistic strategies and literal content in order to assess meaning. The detailed content of items in each of these categories is presented systematically in this chapter and selected items are examined in detail in subsequent chapters.

The 'big' messages are that racism should be exposed in society, that politicians are concerned to win black and minority ethnic votes, that immigrants are suffering in a variety of ways, that minorities are a social problem and that something should be done to both restrict immigration and improve opportunities for minority groups that are here. These messages played differently across different news media.

On the positive side, race news in the tabloids is dominated by items that expose racism of various sorts and they had a higher proportion of items in this category compared to other media. Also, they carried a good proportion of pro-ethnic minority items in General Election coverage, and carried a higher proportion of items which constructed minorities as a social asset than did radio and television. There was little evidence of anti anti-racism items in dramatic comparison to the 1980s, and the tabloids tended to cover fewer items about measures to tackle racism than other media. But, some old problems remain. They are more likely to construct ethnic minorities as a social problem and carry items hostile to immigrants, compared to other media. As a result one-third of race coverage carried a negative message, which is in strong contrast to other media (see Table 2.4).

Despite popular perceptions, about a quarter of broadsheet items tended to carry a negative message about ethnic minorities in the UK. Half of these items covered social problems associated with ethnic minorities. The treatment of these items requires review to assess the extent to which they attribute cause and reproduce an inappropriate 'blame the victim' analysis.

The bulk of radio and television coverage, that is over 80 per cent, was broadly positive in the messages conveyed about ethnic minorities and there was much less evidence of hostile items within the context of a much lower number of items than the papers. Anti-immigrant items and social problem items were in evidence and require review.

Table 2.4   Pro-migrant and anti-migrant messages by media type (%)

Message	Tabloid	Broadsheet	Radio	Television
Immigration				
Pro-immigrant	2.8	7.4	22.4	14.9
Anti-immigrant	11.6	4.3	5.2	4.7
Gen. election				
Pro-minorities	10.0	15.7	9.9	20.9
Anti-minorities	3.4	2.8	0.5	2.7
Racism				
Exposing	44.7	34.2	39.1	35.1
Denying	1.6	2.4	2.6	1.4
Social value				
Assets	3.8	6.5	2.1	0.7
Problems	14.1	12.3	7.8	4.1
M/C Britain				
For	1.9	3.9	2.1	1.4
Against	1.3	1.3	0	0
Opportunities				
Improve	3.1	5.7	5.2	10.8
Restrict	1.3	0.5	0	0
Other	0.6	3.2	3.2	3.4
Total	100	100	100	100
Total hostile anti-migrant	33.3	23.6	16.1	12.9

Detailed composition of race-news messages

Racism and discrimination: expose or deny?

Each of the categories set out in Table 2.3 will be examined in this chapter in relation to the detailed content of news items. The primary message that accounted for almost 38 per cent of news items was that *racism is socially unacceptable*. 'Journalism of attachment', to use Martin Bell's phrase, is particularly evident in the treatment of in-

Table 2.5 Items exposing racism and racial discrimination

Item type	Item count
Stephen Lawrence case	77
Sport racism (in football 65, cricket 2)	67
NHS racism (anti-Abbott 30, pro-Abbott 8, other 17)	55
Police racism (against other police officers 16, against public 27)	43
Armed Forces racism	30
Extreme right (Combat 18 24, propaganda 3, Nazis 2)	29
Ford's racial discrimination	27
Racist attitudes (of whites 17, Asian/Jewish anti-black 5)	22
Anti-semitism	20
Church racism	17
Court racism (by judges 15, juries 1)	16
Racial attacks (on Asians 4, blacks 4, whites 2, increase in 3)	13
Racial discrimination against minorities at work	11
Racial discrimination against whites at work	10
Entertainment racism (in comedy 6, drama 2, television 1)	9
Racial discrimination in fashion industry	9
Education racism (by teachers 4, by pupils 3)	7
Racial discrimination by Japanese firms	6
Racism and BBC Reith lectures	5
Racial discrimination in employment, awards to victims	3
Racial discrimination by airlines	3
Fire Service: racism of staff	2
Racial discrimination by legal services	2
Financial services and racism	2
Voluntary sector organisations and racism	2
Racial discrimination against Gypsies	1
Racial discrimination against Muslims	1
Other	2
Total	491

stances and incidents of racism in the news. Racial attacks, acts of racial discrimination and racist comments made by well-known individuals make the news agenda and they are generally presented as being 'true'. Here, impartiality does not involve detachment from the basic belief that racism is morally wrong. These items form the bulk of race-news coverage and the constant repetition of this message across a range of political, social and institutional contexts must be taken into account in any estimation of the impact of overall 'race' news on the memory of viewers and readers (Table 2.5).

The following examples range from front-page stories to small items and illustrate the tone of the items included in Table 2.5. It is important to note that although a large bulk of material is presented below, it is vital to appreciate the depth, extent and range of these news items. These are also the items which rarely feature in literature on racism in the news media and there can be a tendency to forget or play down the significance of such reporting.

Examples of 'exposing racism' headlines

1. *Racism in the criminal justice system*
    BIGOTS ON THE BEAT (*Mirror*, 3 April 1997)
    POLICE APOLOGISE FOR COMEDIAN'S RACIST ROUTINE (*Guardian*, 19 February 1997)
    HOW I BEAT RACE HATE IN THE FORCE (*Mirror*, 26 March 1997)
    BLACK POLICE OFFICER DENIED 56 PROMOTIONS (*Daily Telegraph*, 2 April 1997)
    ASIAN PC GETS £3,000 IN RACE CASE (*Independent*, 28 March 1997)
    MET. SUED TWICE OVER RACIAL AND SEXUAL HARASSMENT (BBC 2, 27 November 1996)
    BLACK YOUTH DIED IN POLICE CUSTODY (Channel 4 News, 10 April 1997)
    A HAIRDRESSER WAS BEATEN UP AND RACIALLY ABUSED BY POLICE IN LONDON (Radio 1 News, 19 February 1997)
    MURDER MUM SLAMS 'RACIST' LEGAL SYSTEM (*Mirror*, 11 February 1997)
    WHITE JUSTICE FAILED MY SON (*Daily Mail*, 11 February 1997)
    WHY ARE RACE THUGS ALLOWED TO WALK FREE? (*Daily Mail*, 24 March 1997)

UNLAWFULLY KILLED IN AN UNPROVOKED RACIST ATTACK BY FIVE WHITE YOUTHS (*Guardian*, 14 February 1997)

BRITAIN ALLOWS RACE MURDERS, SAYS MOTHER (*Daily Telegraph*, 11 February 1997)

FURY AT JUDGES 'NIGGER' SLUR (*Mirror*, 13 March 1997)

'NIGGER' REMARK JUDGE CARPETED (*Daily Mail*, 27 March 1997)

2. *Employer racism*

BLACK NURSE TELLS OF RACE TAUNTS (*Daily Mail*, 16 April 1997)

NHS RACIST, SAYS ABBOTT (*Guardian*, 16 January 1997)

AFRO-CARIBBEAN'S HIT THE CEMENT ROOF [Building industry racism] (*Guardian*, 7 December 1996)

ALL FIRMS WARNED AFTER £10,000 AWARDS TO 7 IN FORD RACE ROW (*London Evening Standard*, 28 January 1997)

FORDS RACIST RECRUITMENT POLICY (Radio 4, 4 December 1996)

FORDS RACIST RECRUITMENT POLICY (BBC 1, 4 December 1996)

MUSLIM WOMAN APPEALS AGAINST SACKING (*Guardian*, 7 December 1996)

TURBAN TURBULENCE: BRITISH AIRWAYS ACCUSED OF RACISM BY SIKHS (*Daily Mail*, 31 January 1997)

PREJUDICED FASHION BOSSES INSULT ME AS THE BLACK BARDOT (*Sun*, 11 April 1997)

FIREMAN WINS CLAIM OVER RACIST TAUNTS (*The Times*, 26 April 1997)

MUSIC TEACHER COMPLAINS OF 'ORCHESTRATED RACISM' (*Daily Mail*, 11 February 1997)

BLACK VICAR WINS HOSPITAL RACE CASE (*Guardian*, 5 April 1997)

AIRLINES RACIST, SAY SICKLE CELL SUFFERERS (*Sunday Telegraph*, 16 February 1997)

3. *Racism in the community*

WHITE LAD DRIVEN OUT OF HOME BY RACISTS (*Sun*, 15 January 1997)

RACE HATE VICTIM, 11, WINS RIGHT TO MOVE (*Daily Mail*, 14 January 1997)

FAMILIES FORCED TO FLEE ESTATE OF HATE (*Daily Mail*, 21 February 1997)

MAN DROVE AT ASIANS IN RACIST ASSAULT (*The Times*, 8 April 1997)

COUPLE DRIVEN FROM CESSPIT OF RACISM (*Guardian*, 26 April 1997)

4. *Racism in Europe*
    GYPSIES HAVE BECOME THE JEWS OF EUROPE (*Observer*, 1 December 1996)
    EUROPEAN YEAR AGAINST RACISM: NAZI NETWORK IN DENMARK (ITV News, 30 January 1997)
5. *Extreme right racism*
    I STILL SUFFER RACE HATE SAYS VICTIM OF NAZIS (*Yorkshire Evening Post*, 22 February 1997)
    RIGHT-WING MAGAZINE IS RACIST TRASH, SAYS JUDGE (*The Times*, 26 April 1997)
    GERMAN SKINHEADS JAILED FOR ATTACK ON BLACK BRITISH MAN (*Daily Telegraph*, 3 December 1996)
    RACE BOMBERS TARGET STARS (*Daily Mail*, 20 January 1997)
    I WON'T LET RACE BOMBERS DESTROY OUR MARRIAGE (*Daily Mail*, 29 March 1997)
    COMBAT 18 RACISTS JAILED (*The Times*, 13 March 1997)
    NEW MOVE TO CURB RACISTS ON THE INTERNET (*Daily Telegraph*, 20 February 1997)
6. *Racist attitudes*
    YOUNG BRITAIN: BIGOTED, RACIST, BOASTING ABOUT SEX (*London Evening Standard*, 5 February 1997)
    MODERN BRITAIN'S BLEND OF RACISM AND REASON (*London Evening Standard*, 4 February 1997)
    YOU DON'T HAVE TO BE WHITE TO BE A RACIST (*Daily Mail*, 5 February 1997)
    SURVEY REVEALS RACIST STREAK IN ASIANS (*Guardian*, 5 February 1997)
    BRITAIN'S YOUTH THE MOST INTOLERANT IN EUROPE (*Guardian*, 6 February 1997)
    NATION OF SELF-INDULGENT XENOPHOBES (*Independent*, 21 November 1996)
    MORE THAN 90 PER CENT OF BRITISH PEOPLE BELIEVE THE COUNTRY IS RACIST (Radio 1 News, 5 February 1997)
    RACIST RANT? TOO POLITE BY HALF [BBC Reith Lectures] (*Guardian*, 26 February 1997)
7. *Racism in the armed forces*
    OUR RACIST FORCES, BY THE SPIES SENT IN BY THE MINISTRY (*Daily Mail*, 12 March 1997)
    11 SQUADIES TRY TO SCRUB BLACK HERO WHITE (*Sun*, 3 April 1997)

KU KLUX KLAN SHAME OF ARMY JOKES (*Daily Mail*, 20 March 1997)

PREJUDICE ON PARADE (*Daily Mail*, 17 March 1997)

RACISM WIDESPREAD IN ARMED FORCES (*Guardian*, 21 March 1997)

FORCES UNDER FIRE FOR BLIND EYE ON RACISM (*Daily Telegraph*, 21 March 1997)

RACIST ATTITUDES IN ARMY (Radio 4, 3 April 1997)

8. *Racism in sport*

SCHMEICHEL FACES COPS RACE CHARGE (*Mirror*, 21 February 1997)

STONED! SPAT AT! RACE HATE MOB TAUNTS UNITED (*Mirror*, 21 April 1997)

FOOTY BAN ON RACE JIBE YOB (*Sun*, 18 April 1997)

WHY THE BLACK SOCCER STARS ARE PAYING A PENALTY (*Daily Mail*, 7 April 1997)

GROBBELAAR FIGHTS RACISM (*Sunday Independent*, 16 March 1997)

ENGLAND STARS TACKLE RACISTS (*Guardian*, 28 March 1997)

FOOTBALLER REFUSES TO PLAY FOR RACIST WALES MANAGER (*Daily Telegraph*, 2 April 1997)

HOW RACISM DROVE ME OUT OF FOOTBALL (*Observer*, 2 March 1997)

ASIAN CRICKETERS STEREOTYPING (*Independent*, 30 November 1996)

BLACK CRICKETERS CAUGHT OUT BY AN ANCIENT BATTING ORDER (*Sunday Times*, 27 April 1997)

Denials of racism headlines

In contrast there were a group of news messages reporting denials of racism. As Table 2.3 shows, these amounted to 27 items or 2 per cent of all news items, in comparison to 487 or 38 per cent providing reports of the existence of racism. Examples of headlines from these former items include:

WE ARE NOT A NATION OF RACISTS (*Yorkshire Evening Post*, 22 February 1997)

MAJOR DENIES TORY RACISM (*Guardian*, 22 April 1997)

NO-ONE CAN POSSIBLY SAY THAT THE CONSERVATIVE PARTY IS RACIST (BBC 2, 5 March 1997)

DENIAL OF ANTI-SEMITISM, EDITOR APOLOGISES FOR 'JEW RIF-
KIND' REMARK (*Daily Telegraph*, 25 February 1997)
BLUE PETER SWEPT BY POLITICAL CORRECTNESS (*Daily Mail*, 9
May 1997)

Immigration and asylum-seekers: stay or go?

Coverage of immigration and asylum-seeker issues, outside the General Election debates, was more likely to be positive with 8 per cent of
items in this category compared to 6 per cent of anti-immigrant items
(see Table 2.3). But this latter group contained some of the worst
examples of news coverage many of which were firmly placed in the
old frames of the immigrant welfare burden, the need for racialised
control of migrant numbers and cheating, fiddling, conning, fraudulent immigrants. Asylum-seeker and immigration issues emerged as a
dominant theme particularly in the second half of January, accounting
for 37 per cent of items, which compared to 14 per cent of items over
the whole study period. The bulk of the coverage gave voice to critics
and campaigners against government policy and tended to provide
coverage favourable to those asylum-seekers who were on hunger
strike in Rochester Prison. For example, the Channel 4 news item (29
January 1997) reported the views of protesters, the Refugee Council,
Jeremy Corbyn MP, an Anglican clergyman and an academic who all
sided with the asylum-seekers in comparison to a brief comment from
Anne Widdicombe, former Home Office minister. Sky News (1 February 1997) carried criticism from protesters and no government comment. In contrast, the *Sun*'s article (30 January 1997) EAT OR DIE
THREAT TO MIGRANTS gave voice solely to Ann Widdecombe. The
Daily Mail front page WE WON'T SAVE THE HUNGER STRIKERS (30
January 1997) accompanied by a further article, TIME TO SHUT THE
DOOR ON ASYLUM SEEKERS (30 January 1997: 8) endorsed government
policy and commented that, 'we do not want to be swamped by
immigrants', that Britain 'could be swamped by tens of millions of
people with legitimate grounds for claiming asylum' and if so 'any
tradition of tolerance would quickly disappear'. Such views were explicitly criticised in a letter to the *Guardian* (31 January 1997) which ran
under the headline, IT IS RACISM THAT FEEDS OFFICIAL CALLOUSNESS
TO HUNGER STRIKERS. The introduction of employers' obligations to
check passports under the 1996 Asylum and Immigration Act also
received coverage and this was critically reported in the *Independent*,

NO PASSPORT, NO JOB (28 January 1997) which highlighted the
detrimental impact on 'race relations'. A different perspective was
evident in two *Times* editorials, the first, QUESTIONS UNANSWERED, (9
December 1996), contained a negative linkage of 'rabid dogs and
asylum seekers' in the context of criticism of the government's position on EU policy, and the second, RED CROSS BUNGLE (19 December
1996), was strongly critical of the provision of Red Cross food parcels
for asylum-seekers in the UK calling them an 'inefficient' and 'inappropriate response' to poverty and exclusion from benefits.
Clear bias against asylum-seekers was evident in a number of articles;
for example, UNGRATEFUL FED, YOU'D THINK ASYLUM SEEKERS
WOULD BE GRATEFUL FOR ANYTHING (*Sun*, 14 February 1997),
WHO'S RUNNING THE ASYLUM (*Sun*, 14 February 1997), IT'S HARD TO
STOMACH: ASYLUM SEEKERS THREATEN COURT ACTION TO GET
BETTER MEALS ON THE TAXPAYER (*Daily Mail*, 14 February 1997).
Table 2.6 lists the item counts for various pro-and anti-immigrant
messages.

Table 2.6   Competing immigration discourse

Anti-immigrant message	Item count
Reducing migrant rights	22
Welfare burden	19
Conning migrants (e.g. false passports)	11
Supporting immigration policy	8
Confining migrants (e.g. prison/detention)	6
Negative social effects	5
Fiddling migrants (e.g. benefit fraud)	4
Terrorist migrants	3
Numbers increasing	3
Total	81
Pro-immigrant message	
Immigrant/asylum protests	30
Extending migrant rights	22
Attacking immigration policy	18
Migrants welfare needs	15
Plight of migrants	35
Numbers falling	1
Total	121

Examples of anti-immigrant headlines

CHEATING MIGRANTS GRAVE FIDDLE (*News of the World*, 30 March 1997)

DEADMAN WALKING: HE RIPS OFF DSS FROM GRAVE (*News of the World*, 23 March 1997)

WHITEHALL CROOKS LET IN HUNDREDS OF IMMIGRANTS (*Mirror*, 5 April 1997)

WE CATCH 350 MIGRANTS IN WEDDING CON SCANDAL (*News of the World*, 19 January 1997)

YOU PAY, A SCROUNGER STAYS (*Daily Mail*, 15 April 1997)

£250,000 BILL FOR AIDS IMMIGRANT 'TOO ILL TO LEAVE' (*Daily Telegraph*, 15 April 1997)

£40,000 BILL FOR THIEVING MIGRANT (*Daily Mail*, 5 March 1997)

THE HOLES IN A HUNGER STRIKER'S TALE OF WOE (*Daily Mail*, 5 February 1997)

BOGUS REFUGEES WHO PLANE-HOP TO BRITAIN (*Daily Mail*, 7 April 1997)

FREED, THE REFUGEE WHO ABUSED A CHILD (*Daily Mail*, 5 April 1997)

REFUGEES BITE HANDS THAT FEED THEM (*London Evening Standard*, 18 February 1997)

TIME TO SHUT DOOR ON ASYLUM SEEKERS (*Daily Mail*, 30 January 1997)

Examples of pro-immigrant headlines

ORDEAL OF WIDOW SARADA (*Daily Mail*, 29 November 1996)

DESPERATE CARGO (*Independent*, 25 March 1997)

A REFUGEE FROM INDIA WHO STOWED AWAY ON THE UNDERCARRIAGE (Radio 1, 14 March 1997)

CLAMP DOWN ON IMMIGRATION, PLIGHT OF THE FORGOTTEN REFUGEES (Channel 4, 3 December 1996)

HONG KONG 'ASIANS' WIN RIGHT TO HOLD UK PASSPORTS (*Sunday Telegraph*, 4 February 1997)

ETHNIC MINORITIES IN BRITAIN GIVEN BRITISH PASSPORTS (Channel 4, 4 February 1997)

SPARE THE REFUGEES (*London Evening Standard*, 20 February 1997)

SICK HUNGER STRIKE REFUGEE FREED AND 'LEFT WITHOUT HELP' (*Guardian*, 26 February 1997)

CHALLENGE TO ASYLUM LAWS IN TEST CASE (*Daily Telegraph*, 4 February 1997)

ASYLUM SEEKERS WIN RIGHT TO FREE FOOD & SHELTER (*The Times*, 18 February 1997)

STANDING FAST FOR ASYLUM SEEKERS FREEDOM (*Guardian*, 17 February 1997)

RELIGIOUS LEADERS PLEAD FOR INTERVENTION IN HUNGER STRIKE (*Independent*, 31 January 1997)

LAWS ON ASYLUM: PRISON IS NOT THE ANSWER TO BRITAIN'S QUEUES (*The Times*, 31 February 1997)

THE LUNACY OF OUR ASYLUM DEBATE (*Independent*, 6 March 1997)

JAILING ASYLUM SEEKERS FLOUTS HUMAN RIGHTS (*Independent*, 5 February 1997)

General Election race-news coverage: woo the vote or play the race card?

News coverage which linked race to the General Election had an even stronger anti-racist frame than news coverage overall. About 85 per cent of items were broadly positive towards minorities and migrants. The key election frame, which accounted for about 40 per cent of items, was the value and importance of Asian, Muslim and black voters and politicians' attempts to 'woo' them, particularly in marginal constituencies. John Major's bid to 'woo the Asian vote' during and after his visit to Pakistan and India received significant coverage. This attention to race issues early in the pre-Election season was covered in a generally positive fashion. The *Independent*'s leader A SILLY HAT BUT A SOPHISTICATED MESSAGE (15 January 1997), The *Observer*'s leader TEARING UP THE RACE CARD and related article, MAJOR RISES ABOVE MOCKERY IN BID TO BECOME MAN FOR ALL RACES (19 January 1997) and the *Mirror*'s cartoon WELL IT WORKED FOR GHANDI (11 January 1997) exemplify this press reaction. In contrast, front page coverage in the *Guardian*, WHAT A MAJOR CARRY-ON UP THE KHYBER (14 January 1997) and the *Mirror*, THE KHYBER ASS was left with little to do but ridicule what was, after all, a multicultural image of John Major in an Afghan turban. Significant credit must go to John Major in that, firstly, coverage of his efforts to gain Asian votes received most coverage. Secondly, his silencing of Budgen's and Howard's (*Telegraph*, 26 April 1997) attempts to make racialised immigration policy election news led to a significant downturn in media interest in 'race' items. ('Race' items dropped to their lowest weekly level in 1997 during the week 24–30 March). This was aided by Tony Blair whose silence on race, support for Major's position on keeping race off the election agenda, and rare support for anti-racist policies was reflected in news coverage. There were 18 items (9 per cent of race and election coverage) which actively demanded that racialised immigration policy should be election news and 10 items (5 per cent) that called for these issues to be kept off the agenda (Table 2.7). The call for putting anti-racism on the agenda was acknowledged in only four items.

Table 2.7   General Election discourse

Anti-minorities message	Item count
John Major should 'play the race card'	18
Voters express 'Dinner Party' racism	8
Supports racist views of Conservative MP	5
Anti-black views of Conservative voters	8
Labour Party racism	2
John Major opposes Euro anti-racism	1
Total	42

Pro-minorities message	
John Major woos Asian vote	28
Opposing the extreme right (BNP)	23
Condemns racist views of Conservative MP	21
Importance of Asian vote	22
Importance of black vote	16
Keep race out of the election	10
Criticisms of racism in political parties	10
Importance of Muslim vote	9
Labour and prospective black/Asian MPs	9
Supporting anti-racism	5
Concern over low black (youth) vote	5
Jewish support for Tony Blair	5
Lib. Democrats' support for ethnic minorities	4
Condemning voters' racism	4
Significance of ethnicity for voting	3
Labour will ease immigration controls	3
Launch of 'ethnic' issues Party	2
Criticism of Labour immigration record	2
John Major's multicultural origins	1
Black parliamentary candidates	1
Total	183

A significant level of debate and protest was generated over the broadcasting of the BNP election address. This was banned by Channel 4 due to its infringement of Independent Television guidelines in showing identifiable black people, whose permission had not been requested, with the commentary 'Do you want the rest of Britain to end up like this?' News coverage of this debate gave voice to anti-racist groups but did not give an opportunity for a reply by the BNP, and implicit opposition to racism underlay much of this coverage. Yet, curtailment of the freedom and opportunity to incite racial hatred in discussion of the pros and cons of this item did not stifle this debate and there is little likelihood that banning the BNP broadcast would have had a similar effect. These issues were discussed in a 'Head to Head' debate between Michael Mansfield and Donu Kogbara in the *Guardian* (19 April 1997). Mansfield argued against broadcasting messages which incite racial hatred particularly because of the link to racial violence, and Kogbara argued against censorship and for allowing viewers to judge for themselves. Concern was also voiced, and reported, from black and Asian people over Labour's use of a bulldog in an election broadcast due to its associations with the far-right and British imperialism.

Examples of General Election headlines

1. *Calls to 'play the race card'*
    TORIES PUT MIGRANTS ON ELECTION AGENDA (*Daily Mail*, 19 March 1997)
    WHY WON'T JOHN MAJOR LET THE COMMONS DEBATE IMMIGRATION (*Daily Mail*, 13 March 1997)
    WHY IS MAJOR RUNNING SCARED OF THE R-WORD? (*News of the World*, 16 March 1997)
    TORY MP SAYS RACE IS ISSUE FOR VOTERS (*Daily Telegraph*, 2 March 1997)
    IMMIGRATION IS AN ISSUE (*Daily Telegraph*, 12 March 1997)
    REDWOOD SUPPORTS RIGHT TO CAMPAIGN OVER RACE (*The Times*, 26 March 1997)
    WE IGNORE IMMIGRATION AT OUR PERIL (*The Times*, 18 March 1997)
    THE TORY POLICY THAT MR MAJOR WILL NOT SUPPORT (*The Times*, 13 March 1997)

HOW LONG SHALL WE AVOID THE IMMIGRATION ISSUE? (*Independent*, 27 March 1997)

A DEBATE THE PARTIES DENIED US (*Daily Telegraph*, 30 April 1997)

2. *Calls not to 'play the race card'*

RACE CARD SOURS DEBATE (*Guardian*, 14 April 1997)

BLAIR PRAISES MAJOR OVER RACE POLICY (*Daily Telegraph*, 5 March 1997)

RACE IS NO LONGER A BLACK & WHITE ISSUE, SAY VOTERS (*Daily Telegraph*, 21 March 1997)

HOWARD IS SILENCED ON IMMIGRATION (*Daily Telegraph*, 26 April 1997)

MAIN PARTY LEADERS AGREE TO KEEP RACE OUT OF THE ELECTION (Channel 4, 10 April 1997)

3. *The importance of wooing the ethnic minority vote*

ISSUES OF IMPORTANCE TO ETHNIC MINORITIES IN CARDIFF (Radio 4, 28 April 1997)

9/10 YOUNG BLACKS WILL NOT VOTE (*London Evening Standard*, 8 January 1997)

BLACK VOTERS TARGETED IN ELECTION DRIVE (*Independent*, 10 February 1997)

MAJOR BID FOR VOTES. . . . . IN INDIA (*Mirror*, 10 January 1997)

JOIN US, MAJOR URGES ASIANS (*Sunday Mirror*, 19 January 1997)

PM'S LATEST ATTEMPT TO CURRY FAVOUR (*News of the World*, 12 January 1997)

MAJOR WOOS ETHNIC VOTERS, BUT ADMITS RACISM EXISTS (*Sunday Independent*, 19 January 1997)

TORY MP URGES ACTION TO WOO ASIAN VOTERS (*Guardian*, 26 February 1997)

TORIES STRUGGLE TO LOSE RACIST IMAGE IN KEY MARGINALS (*Guardian*, 10 January 1997)

CAMPAIGNING MAJOR PRAISES ASIAN VALUES (*Daily Telegraph*, 10 January 1997)

MAJOR RISES ABOVE MOCKERY IN BID TO BECOME A MAN OF ALL RACES (*Observer*, 19 January 1997)

TEARING UP THE RACE CARD (*Observer*, 19 January 1997)

ETHNIC MINORITY VALUES ARE TORY VALUES (BBC 1, 18 January 1997)

HOW TO GET THE BLACK VOTE BACK (*Guardian*, 11 January 1997)

LABOUR'S WHITE SUITS TURN OFF BLACK VOTERS (*Independent*, 12 April 1997)

BLACK COMMUNITY PLAY RACE CARD ON LABOUR (*Independent*, 29 April 1997)

ELECTION CAMPAIGNING-GAINING BLACK VOTE (Channel 4, 14 February 1997)

GENERAL ELECTION AND ETHNIC MINORITY ISSUES (Radio 4, 14 January 1997)

PARTIES WARNED TO COURT MUSLIMS OR FACE TROUBLE (*Guardian*, 21 February 1997)

MOSQUES ISSUE GUIDELINE FOR 1.5 M MUSLIM VOTERS (*Daily Telegraph*, 28 January 1997)

LABOUR WARNED OF LOST MUSLIM VOTES (*The Times*, 4 March 1997)

BLACK BRITAIN AND LABOUR, FOR BETTER OR WORSE (*Guardian*, 11 February 1997)

LABOUR PARTY ATTEMPTING TO GAIN ASIAN VOTE & MPS (Radio 4, 15 February 1997)

THE BATTLE FOR THE ASIAN VOTE HEATS UP (*London Evening Standard*, 19 February 1997)

HOWARD HITS THE TEMPLE TRAIL (*The Times*, 9 April 1997)

PARTIES BREAK NEW GROUND WITH TV APPEAL TO ASIANS (*The Times*, 12 April 1997)

ASIAN VOTERS COULD DECIDE ON THE OUTCOME OF UP TO 36 SEATS (BBC 1, 29 April 1997)

THE ASIAN COMMUNITY IN BRITAIN IS BEING TARGETED BY POLITICIANS (Sky News, 11 April 1997)

ETHNIC ISSUES PARTY LAUNCHED (*Guardian*, 2 April 1997)

4. *Opposing anti-racism*

MAJOR VETOS RACISM FIGHT (*Guardian*, 27 January 1997)

5. *Opposing racism*

BLAIR BACKS COOK ON RACISM GIBE (*The Times*, 10 March 1997)

RACE: WHEN LABOUR HAD TO BACKTRACK (*Daily Telegraph*, 17 March 1997)

ANTI-RACIST MEASURES PROMISED BY BLAIR (*Independent*, 25 April 1997)

LET'S INTRODUCE A QUOTA SYSTEM FOR XENOPHOBIA (*Guardian*, 17 April 1997)

MAJOR PLEDGES FIGHT AGAINST RACISM (*Guardian*, 20 February 1997)

MAJOR URGED TO REBUKE TORY MP IN 'RACE SLUR' (*Yorkshire Evening Post*, 5 March 1997)
LOONY TORY'S A CLONE DANGER (*Mirror*, 10 March 1997)
MAJOR RAGING WITH FURY AT BIG MOUTH (*Sun*, 6 March 1997)
JOHN MAJOR HAS UNRESERVEDLY CONDEMNED REMARKS BY THE CONS. MP (BBC 1, 5 March 1997)
LABOUR BANS RACIST BULLDOG (*Sunday Telegraph*, 20 April 1997)
BERNIE GRANT HAS A BONE TO PICK OVER BULLDOG FITZ (*Daily Telegraph*, 29 April 1997)

6. *Racist views of voters*
EAT, DRINK, BE BIGOTED. TOMORROW WE VOTE (*Guardian*, 13 March 1997)
WE'RE NOT ASHAMED OF OUR VIEWS, SAY TV DINNER GUESTS (*The Times*, 14 March 1997)
RACIST TABLE TALK OF MIDDLE ENGLAND (*Independent*, 14 March 1997)

7. *BNP items*
THIS MAN IS A US NAZI, HE IS HELPING THE BNP (*Independent*, 2 March 1997)
HOW THE BNP DIVIDES (*Guardian*, 22 April 1997)
DON'T PLUG RACISM (*Independent*, 24 April 1997)
ANTI RACIST GROUPS DEMONSTRATE OUTSIDE BBC BROADCASTING HOUSE (Radio 4, 25 April 1997)

8. *Call for racial justice agenda*
RACE FOR THE ELECTION (advert in *Guardian*, 17 April 1997)

9. *Increased minority ethnic representation in Parliament*
MINORITIES JOIN RECORD NUMBER OF WOMEN MP'S (*The Times*, 3 May 1997)

Minority groups: social problem or a national asset?

In general, minority ethnic groups tend to be constructed as a social problem in the news rather than as a social asset, as Table 2.8 shows. The dominant theme here is the linkage to crime news, which, as noted above, may or may not be legitimate in the context of a particular item, for example, NIGERIAN'S TOP UK'S FRAUD LEAGUE (*Independent*, 29 April 1997). The triple linkage of crime, race and sex in rape cases generated the greatest amount of coverage in this group, for example TROPHY RAPE BY TEENAGE JACKALS (*Daily Mail*, 12 April 1997). The unusual story which reported on the stereotyping of all beggars as Scottish also produced substantial coverage. The wider social problems faced by minority ethnic groups such as housing, ill-health, and poor educational and social welfare provision received very little coverage, with such issues accounting for only 10 per cent of all social problem items. Whereas, the problems seen to be caused by minorities themselves were given much greater coverage, for example CRYING KIDS FLEE AS MUSLIM SIR RANTS AT CAROLS (*Mirror*, 19 December 1996).

In contrast, the contribution of Asian and black people to the creation of wealth, the provision of entertainment and the world of

Table 2.8 Messages about the presence of minority ethnic groups in society

Social problem messages	Item count
Link to rape	30
Involvement in other crime	27
(drugs, fraud, prostitution, murder etc.)	
Group violence	18
(riots 7, Sikh/Muslim 7, policing 3, feuds 1)	
Scottish beggars	17
Problems in adoption/fostering	14
Causing problems in education	13
(Muslim outburst 9, exclusion 3, absenteeism 1)	
Causing divided cities / ghettos	7
Public expenditure burden	6
(comm. projects, equality initiatives etc.)	
Health issues	5
Homelessness	3
Asian family issues	3
Total	143
Social asset messages	
Entertainment achievements	19
(pop, theatre, film, dance, jazz, literature, comedy, fashion)	
Asian and black economic enterprise	18
Sporting achievements	11
Blacks in senior positions	4
(Bar Council, House of Lords, royal's ancestry)	
Contribution to multicultural city life	4
Jewish contribution to society	2
Total	58

sport were repeatedly acknowledged. These individual contributions received much wider coverage than the contributions of groups of different minorities to social life in the UK.

Examples of 'minority social problem' headlines

POLICE 'MUST EARN ASIAN TRUST' IN RIOT CITY (*Guardian*, 21 November 1996)

BLACKS AND RIOTS (Radio 4, 14 January 1997)

SOUTHHALL SIKHS ATTACK MUSLIMS IN FEUD (*Independent*, 28 April 1997)

ASIAN VS. ASIAN AS 'KHALISTAN' ROW STRIKES UK (*Independent*, 4 May 1997)

POVERTY & DESPAIR BEHIND A WAR OF ASIAN GANGS (*Guardian*, 3 May 1997)

OUR DUTY TO DEMOLISH GHETTO WALLS (*Observer*, 16 March 1997)

RACE RELATIONS MUST AVOID GHETTOS (*Daily Telegraph*, 27 January 1997)

WELCOME TO ENGLAND'S LAST COLONY (*Guardian*, 30 November 1996)

GANG RAPE OF WHITE TOURIST WAS RACIST: QC (*Sun*, 10 April 1997)

GANGSTERS EXPLOIT POLICE RACE FEARS (*Sunday Telegraph*, 16 March 1997)

NIGERIAN'S TOP UK'S FRAUD LEAGUE (*Independent*, 29 April 1997)

CASH GOES MISSING IN BLACK CHURCHES (*Independent*, 30 April 1997)

BLACK STUDENTS ON THE END OF SCHOOL EXPULSIONS (*Independent*, 26 November 1996)

CRYING KIDS FLEE AS MUSLIM SIR RANTS AT CAROLS (*Mirror*, 19 November 1996)

MUSLIM TEACHER TAKES MUSLIM CHILDREN OUT OF CHRISTIAN CELEBRATION (Radio 4, 19 December 1996)

ISLINGTON ECHOES (funding and black needs) (*Daily Mail*, 13 December 1996)

GRANTS GALORE IF YOU ARE GAY [refugee funding] (*Daily Mail*, 18 December 1996)

£164 M GRANT FOR HINDU COMMUNITY (*Daily Telegraph*, 20 November 1996)

TWO FACED INQUIRY ON ETHNIC GRANTS (*Daily Telegraph*, 3 December 1996)

RACE BIAS 'IGNORANCE' RULED COUPLE OUT (*Daily Telegraph*, 18 February 1997)

TWO-EDGED CASE ON RACISM AND MADNESS (*Independent*, 14 December 1996)

MOST BEGGARS ARE SCOTTISH (*Daily Mail*, 11 January 1997)

HEY JIMMY: HEARD ABOUT THE MINISTER WHO THINKS MOST BEGGARS ARE SCOTTISH (*Independent*, 11 January 1997)

COURT SPLITS SIKH FAMILY (*The Times*, 30 April 1997)

Examples of 'minorities as a social asset' headlines

BLACK BARRISTER'S DOUBLE FIRST (*Independent*, 31 January 1997)

BANGLATOWN: THE HEART OF THE EAST END (*London Evening Standard*, 23 January 1997)

BID TO ADD CARIBBEAN FEEL TO GREENWICH CELEBRATIONS (*London Evening Standard*, 7 February 1997)

CURRY IS THE HOT TIP AS BRITAIN'S NATIONAL DISH (*Daily Telegraph*, 7 January 1997)

BY ANY STANDARDS OF ALL THE GROUPS IN BRITAIN, ASIAN PEOPLE (AND WEALTH) (Radio 4, 5 March 1997)

WHY HER MAJESTY REALLY IS THE AFRICAN QUEEN (*Sunday Mirror*, 16 March 1997)

ASIAN TIGERS AT LARGE IN BRITAIN (*Guardian*, 8 April 1997)

UNSTOPPABLE RISE OF THE ASIAN RICH IN BRITAIN (*Daily Telegraph*, 19 February 1997)

WEALTHY ASIANS MUST HELP OUT (*Daily Telegraph*, 21 February 1997)

ASIANS PUT RICHES DOWN TO THATCHERITE VALUES, (*The Times*, 19 February 1997)

HE'S 20, WORTH £27 M. HAIL NEW ASIAN TIGER (*Observer*, 16 February 1997)

ASIANS RACE UP LIST OF BRITAIN'S RICHEST (*Sunday Times*, 16 February 1997)

YOUNG, GIFTED AND ASIAN: THE NEW TYCOONS (*Independent*, 16 February 1997)

BLACK MIDDLE CLASS ON THE MOVE (*Sunday Times*, 24 November 1996)

WOODS BREAKS THE MOULD TO THREATEN WORLD DOMINATION (*Daily Telegraph*, 15 April 1997)
TIGER'S SUCCESS MAY MAKE CLUBS CHANGE THEIR STRIPES (*The Times*, 15 April 1997)
INDIAN FILM DIRECTOR SETTING UP STUDIO IN SCOTLAND (Radio 4, 3 December 1996)
ASIAN POP MUSIC (*Daily Telegraph*, 7 December 1996)
ASIAN THEATRE-ITS PLACE IN THE COMMUNITY (*Guardian*, 29 January 1997)
STEPS INTO BLACK HISTORY (*Guardian*, 15 April 1997)

Taking action: improving or restricting opportunities?

Action to tackle racism, racial inequalities, racial discrimination and the promotion of multiculturalism received substantial news coverage. The range of items indicates a depth of concern to publicise such work, and it appears that advocating problems is not as newsworthy as doing something about 'it' (Table 2.4). In contrast, there was a marked lack of items criticising anti-racism which shows a significant change to news in the 1980s.

Examples of 'improving minority opportunities' headlines

NEW BILL TO COVER ALL FORMS OF HARASSMENT (*Daily Telegraph*, 6 December 1996)
EXTRA SCHOOL LESSONS FOR ASIANS AND AFRO-CARIBBEANS (*Independent*, 16 December 1996)
MUSLIM SCHOOLS WIN BACKING (*Independent*, 7 January 1997)
ETON COMES TO TERMS WITH THE HOLOCAUST (*Daily Telegraph*, 22 February 1997)
VIDEO PACK IS LAUNCHED TO TACKLE SCHOOL RACISTS (*Yorkshire Evening Post*, 9 April 1997)
MIXED FAITHS CAN HELP MARRIAGES (*Independent*, 12 December 1996)
GRANT WANTS MEMORIAL TO SLAVES (*Guardian*, 3 March 1997)
20 YEARS OF THE RACE RELATIONS ACT (BBC 1, 21 November 1996)
RACE TO CREATE ETHNIC BALANCE IN THE BOARDROOM (*Guardian*, 1 February 1997)

RACE EQUALITY WILL HELP UK TO COMPETE (*The Times*, 6 January 1997)

EUROPE MUST ACT AGAINST RACISM (*Independent*, 7 January 1997)

POLICE SET OUT TO ATTRACT ETHNIC RECRUITS (*Yorkshire Evening Post*, 5 February 1997)

LETS KICK RACISM EVEN HARDER [Campaign Against racism in Football] (*Guardian*, 5 April 1997)

Table 2.9 Doing something about 'it': intervention discourses

Improving opportunities	Item count
Race relations legislation	15
Improving minorities' educational outcomes	11
Anti-racist education	6
Pro-European anti-racism	5
Tackling racial violence (Stalking Bill)	5
Holocaust education	4
Improving law and order (streetwatch)	4
Inter-faith action	3
Police recruitment	3
Pro-race equality	3
Anti-zero tolerance	3
Historical reparations	2
Tackling football racism	2
Reviewing whitecentric drama	2
Multicultural education	1
Equal opportunities at work	1
Muslim schools	1
Mother tongue education	1
Total	72

Restricting opportunities	
Anti-CRE / costs of racial equality	2
Anti-multicultural education	2
Anti-historical reparation	1
Anti-taking racism into account in court sentencing	1
BNP office location	1
Total	7

Examples of anti anti-racism headlines

HOW RACE ROW ZEALOTS PROMOTE RACISM [attack on Commission
for Racial Equality] (*Daily Mail*, 29 November 1996)
A CITY'S £1.6M HIGH COST OF EQUALITY [criticism of local authority racial equality policies] (*Daily Mail*, 12 January 1997)
DISTURBING GUIDE TO SENTENCING [criticism of guidelines for the
inclusion of consideration of racial motive in court sentences] (*Daily
Telegraph*, 8 April 1997)

Mono- or multicultural Britain?

This group of items conveys a generally positive view of multiculturalism. Much of the debate here has been over the influence of Islam and
the balance of coverage was decidedly positive. The intervention by
Prince Charles into this debate combined with publication of the
Runnymede Trust's Islamophobia report have been significant factors
here. Debate over the reality and extent of national and racial differences between the Scots and the English due particularly to an indus-

Table 2.10   Contesting Britishness

Pro-multicultural UK	Item count
Valuing Islam	15
Scottish identity	9
Valuing Black Britishness	2
Multi-cultural cities	2
Cornish identity	1
Rastafarians	1
Pro-Asian	1
Other	5
Total	36
Anti-multicultural UK	
Anti-Islam	6
Scots / English racial divisions	3
Exclusive Britishness	2
Other	1
Total	12

trial tribunal case was a secondary theme. There was little evidence of xenophobia in these items. Table 2.10 lists the item counts for the pro- and anti-multicultural UK messages.

Examples of 'anti-multicultural UK' headlines

DIVIDED WE STAND (*Sunday Telegraph*, 12 January 1997)

SHOULD WE GUARD AGAINST ISLAMOPHOBIA? (*Daily Mail*, 4 March 1997)

ISLAMIC HORROR, (*Daily Mail*, 6 March 1997)

FAY WELDON HITS BACK AT THE ISLAMICALLY CORRECT (*Independent*, 2 March 1997)

RESIDENTS SIGN UP TO FIGHT PLAN FOR ISLAMIC CENTRE (*Yorkshire Evening Post*, 3 April 1997)

Examples of 'pro-multicultural UK' headlines

RASTAS DO THEIR BIT TO GIVE PRINCE A LIFT OFF (*Guardian*, 3 March 1997)

WHY CHARLES IS DRIVEN TO BUILD A BRIDGE TO THE EAST (*Daily Mail*, 6 January 1997)

PRINCE SEEKS END TO 'ISLAMOPHOBIA' (*Daily Telegraph*, 1 March 1997)

PRINCE CHARLES-DEFENDER OF (ISLAMIC) FAITH (*Daily Telegraph*, 12 December 1996)

BUILDERS ANSWER ISLAM'S GROWING CALL TO PRAYER (*Independent*, 4 February 1997)

WHAT WE LOVE ABOUT LONDON BLACKS (*London Evening Standard*, 19 November 1996)

BLACKS FEEL MORE BRITISH (*Independent*, 18 November 1996)

OUR DUTY TO DEMOLISH GHETTO WALLS (*Observer*, 16 March 1997)

Case study summary

News coverage analysed in this study shows the dominance of an anti-racist agenda. Three-quarters of items were concerned to expose and criticise racist attitudes, statements, actions and policies; to address the concerns of immigrant and minority ethnic groups; to show their contribution to British society; and embraced an inclusive view of multicultural British identity.

The dominant interpretative frame, or central organising idea for making sense of events and suggesting what is at issue (Gamson, 1989: 35), is that racism is wrong (38 per cent of items covered instances of racial attacks, racial discrimination and racist attitudes).

The primary theme in news coverage is crime (16 per cent of items). Here, there are continued irrelevant references to race and ethnicity in crime items, and there is also clear evidence of anti-racist crime reporting. Immigration and asylum-seeker items were on balance critical of government policy and supportive of protesters emphasising the importance of extending rights and meeting needs (8 per cent of items). Racist immigration discourse persisted in 6 per cent of items overall. General Election coverage was broadly positive, the main topic being 'wooing the ethnic minority vote'. There were a small number of items (18) which called for a racialised immigration policy to be put on the agenda, and an even smaller number which called for debate on anti-racist, racial equality and multicultural policies.

Ethnic minorities were constructed as a social problem in 11 per cent of items compared to coverage of their social contribution in 4.5 per cent of items. The real social problems faced by these groups such as housing, ill-health and poor educational and social welfare provision received very little coverage. Individual contributions to the creation of wealth, the provision of entertainment and the world of sport were given much wider coverage than the contributions of groups of different minorities to social life in the UK.

Items that dealt with taking action about race-related problems gave much greater coverage to anti-racist and multicultural measures and there was very little evidence of anti anti-racism, in distinct comparison to the 1980s. Items that dealt with wide discussion of aspects of multiculturalism in the UK were broadly positive, with a significant cluster emphasising the value of Islam.

A third of tabloid items and a quarter of broadsheet items tended to carry a negative message about ethnic minorities. Anti-immigrant items and social problem items require review across all media sources.

Conclusion

In reply to the 'case to answer', set out earlier in this chapter, this case study has shown that in broad terms news coverage is not guilty, due to significant changes in news reporting of race over the last twenty years. The case for the defence rests on acknowledging that *in just under three-quarters of news items a broadly anti-racist message was conveyed.* No explicit racist messages in cartoons were found; hostility to race-relations bureaucracies in central and local government, in particular the ridiculing of anti-racist policies and practices, had largely disappeared; immigration was more likely to be treated in a sympathetic and humanitarian fashion overall; and the former press silence on black people as victims of violence no longer exists. In addition, there is little coverage denying the existence of racism, whereas there is substantial coverage documenting instances of racism and cases of racial discrimination. Politicians rarely articulated 'new racism' involving naturalised hostility to other groups founded on fixed essentialised notions of cultural difference (rather than invocation of racial hierarchies). Multiculturalism and Islam were more likely to be valued than vilified in news articles. In the USA it has also been acknowledged that there has been a radical change in news coverage since the 1970s with a marked shift towards a 'more diverse, socially beneficial (and "accurate") construction of Blacks in the news' (Entman and Rojecki, 2000: 140).

A fuller discussion of anti-racism in news coverage is given in Chapter 4. In addition to these key findings, later chapters will also show how access of minority voices and use of terminology has improved and that deliberate bias against minorities was rare. However, the news media does not have a clean bill of health and a series of problem areas remain.

The case for the prosecution is substantiated by recognition of the dogged staying power of racially hostile news as *a quarter of items continued to convey a negative message about minority groups.* Irrelevant negative references to race and ethnicity are still used, and there are many examples of poor professional practice in the use of group terms which reflects a lack of understanding. The linkage of race, violence, dangerousness and crime remains a constant high-profile theme. The 'old frames' persist, that is immigrants are a welfare burden and are prone to deception hence racialised control, surveillance and expulsion are vital. Support for populist racism, jingoism, chauvinism

and Islamophobia was evident. Also, minorities are frequently constructed as a social problem with little attention to real social welfare
issues amongst minority ethnic communities, for example homelessness, poor housing conditions, education, community care, and so
forth.

Overall, *the diversity of roles that minority groups played in British
news was narrow and limited as they were presented primarily as either
victims of racism and discrimination, perpetrators of crime or problematised immigrants.* This thin repertoire is paralleled in the most recent
study of US news where black people are predominantly seen in
reports as sports figures, entertainers or objects of discrimination,
framing blacks as a culturally/racially distinct group (Entman and
Rojecki, 2000: 64). Through the 1990s the USA has witnessed a shift
to more sensational network news coverage, and in this context representation of blacks has also been seen to have deteriorated with a
sharpening of the narrow focus on blacks as criminals and sports
personalities and a reduced showing of blacks in policy-orientated or
political roles (*ibid.*: 66).

This chapter has demonstrated a significant change in news coverage
of race issues since the 1980s in the UK. However, this '*great anti-racist
show*' may also be seen as an outward, empty attempt of mere display
masking continuing normative and progressive whiteness in news organisations, racial and ethnic inequalities of power and employment,
and a collective failure to provide appropriate quality news services for
black and minority ethnic communities and consumers. Such a 'show'
may well, therefore, be playing against a backcloth of institutional
racism. An examination of how 'unwitting prejudice', the rationale
for institutional racism, may be revealed in the substantial if not
dominant group of negative, hostile news messages is carried out in
the next chapter.

3

Bashing the Bias: Rape, Migration and Naming

Introduction

The news media, particularly the press, selectively repeat, rework and reinvent a simple pattern of key racist messages which have 'helped to build a respectable, coherent, common-sense whiteness' (Gabriel, 1998: 188):

- Minority ethnic groups are violent, dangerous and crime-prone; e.g. BRITAIN FACING ASIAN CRIME WAVE (*The Times*, 3 September 1999);
- Immigrants and asylum-seekers are cheating, fiddling, conning, fraudulent 'leeches on the welfare state' (*Daily Mail*, 12 April, 1997).

This chapter will seek to examine presentation of these themes in more detail looking at coverage of race and rape, immigrants and asylum-seekers, deliberate forms of racial bias in the news and the naming of social groups using racial and ethnic terms.

The fundamental problems with sociological analyses of race in the media established so far are twofold. Firstly, many studies operate within a 'dominance paradigm' (McNair, 1998). This perspective emphasises that the news media play a vital role as producers of a 'dominant discourse', which 'serves dominant social interests' (Fiske, 1996: 5), which disseminates dominant values and which serves to maintain material inequalities, particularly those of class, gender, ethnicity and disability. As the analysis in Chapter 2 established, news media are becoming increasingly open to a plurality of views and positions on race issues with a marked shift, a relative improvement, in the decade between the mid-1980s and the mid-1990s. There are a complex of factors which account for this process including changing cultural, political and government discourse over race issues, changes in minority ethnic employment profile in some news organisations, increasing recognition of anti-racism and multiculturalism in regulatory environments and competitive rivalry in news production (Cottle, 1997, 1999). Lastly, the space, however heavily constrained, which is available for strategies of resistance to racism in the news media including claims for more effective representation of ethnic diversity in both content and staffing, editorial and professional regulation and anti-racist political leadership also indicates the more open and contested nature of news coverage of race than this structural account would suggest.

Secondly, the overriding concern of much sociological analysis has been to identify, evaluate and criticise the ways in which journalism and news production operate in reporting race issues. The review of the news media's 'case to answer' over treatment and coverage of race in Chapter 2 illustrated the detailed ways in which this critique has been developed. The concern to 'bash the bias' in news coverage, although a vital and urgent task, permits, at best, only a partial and limited assessment of news processes, and, at worst, produces poor sociological analysis which is misleading, shallow and distorted. A one-sided selective emphasis on racialised dominant discourse can easily lead to ignoring those news items that do not 'fit' and a downplaying of both the human agency of journalists and audiences, and the real opportunities available for minority ethnic individuals and organisations to influence and improve news coverage. The wider issue of providing a thorough measurement and evaluation of bias in news output raises a series of questions which also require attention (Gunter, 1997). Before engaging with these questions, however, an example is provided below of a recent debate over the extent to which news and television documentary has produced a new stereotype; the 'young black gang-banger'.

Race, rape and crime

Black gang-bangers and the Muslim underclass

The regular linkage of race with rape is a key feature of news coverage that deals with social problems in and amongst minority ethnic groups in the UK. In the content analysis of news coverage across media sources described in the previous chapter, from November 1996 to May 1997, 30 news items were identified which made this link. These items constituted only 2 per cent of overall race-related news coverage, whereas they accounted for 20 per cent of items that reported social problems, particularly crime, amongst minority ethnic groups and they were the largest category in this group. The opportunity for news agencies to create sensational items about race, violence and sexuality was provided by the trial of a gang of eight youths of various ethnicities, some only 14 years old, who were accused and found guilty of raping a white Austrian tourist during April 1997.

In this case, legitimate reference to race was made as the prosecuting QC reported that the attack was 'overtly racist in nature' and that repeated references were made to the 'white bitch' (GANG-RAPE OF WHITE TOURIST WAS RACIST: QC, *Sun*, 10 April 1997). The racist nature of the case was consistently reported but news media varied in their identification of the ethnic origin of the offenders indicating both ambivalence as to the significance of this and also uncertainty in the use of racial and ethnic terms. Television and radio coverage generally chose not to refer to the ethnicity of the gang. The *Independent* referred to only one of the youths as black (10 April 1997), whereas a number of other papers chose to report the prosecuting counsel's reference to the gang as 'mixed-race'. The *Daily Mail*, the *Mirror* and the *Daily Telegraph* printed pictures of all the gang members, and went into greater detail and comment on the significance of race, for example in the item FACES OF EVIL, *Daily Mail*, 14 April 1997. In these pictures, although the gang-members' eyes were blocked out due to reporting restrictions, strong visual clues were given as to their ethnicity for the readers. These reports noted that the gang included immigrants from the Philippines and Colombia, and the British-born children of Caribbean and Greek Cypriot parents. They were led by a '6ft 2in tall', '14 year old of West Indian background'. The *Mirror* makes a point of referring to his 'rippling muscles'. The *Mail* chose to make a comparison between generations of migrants in sweeping stereotypical fashion (12 April 1997). Earlier generations had 'trooped off the boats looking earnestly for work, and shoved their children's head into school books'. These migrants had 'cherished their respectability'. Whereas now migrants came to 'feed like leeches off the welfare state'. Comparisons were also drawn with an American case of the 'Central Park Jogger' where a 'young white woman was raped and left to die' by a

gang of 'blacks and Hispanics'. The prolonged coverage, frequent use
of the front page and the extent and depth of items characterised
tabloid coverage. Would a white gang have been given such treatment?
Would a white gang have been pointedly identified as such and reference made to the significance of their racial and ethnic background,
and the background of their parents and grandparents? If no, then the
difference between the coverage in different news media cannot be
accounted for by different news conventions across television, radio
and the press, and is highly likely to reflect conscious decisions of
editorial choice. This involves conscious decisions to 'play up the
race card' in news coverage and to reinforce stereotypical linkages
between notions of race, sexuality and violence. In comparison, it is
important to note that there was a 'silence' in the news about the rape
and domestic violence suffered by minority ethnic women in the UK.
This parallels findings in America (Meyers, 1997, see below).

More recent coverage of such issues in relation to Asian women is
indicative of a more general trend of portraying linkages between
Asians, violence and crime in the news. *The Times* in a recent front
page refers to the 'shattering' of the belief that Asians are more law-
abiding and that the expected 'upsurge in criminal activity' could lead
to a new 'moral panic' in the country (3 September 1999). In the same
edition, *The Times* in its leading article EAST SIDE STORY, THE
TROUBLED YOUTH OF BRITAIN'S ASIAN MUSLIMS seeks to explain the
'Asian crime wave' by reference to the 'population bulge' of Asian
young men, low academic achievement amongst some Pakistanis and
Bangladeshis, 'ill-equipped' parents and the 'natural temptations' of
juvenile delinquency. Prison statistics from 1997 are used to highlight
both that the largest group of offences committed by male Asians were
either violent or sexual in nature (30%), and racial and ethnic differen-
tials in rates of incarceration. The figures quoted could, however, be
given a completely different interpretation and could equally justify
headlines such as; White Justice Fails Black and Pakistani Communities, or White Crime Wave Engulfs Asian Communities. The figures
show 101 Bangladeshis are imprisoned per 100 000 population compared to 176 whites, 278 Pakistanis and 1249 blacks. The dramatic
difference in incarceration of blacks does not rate a phrase, comment
or any discussion. Given the research and criticism of racism in policing, probation and sentencing of blacks which leads to differential
outcomes in the prison population, this data could have prompted
reporting and analysis of institutional racism faced by Pakistanis in

the criminal justice system. Indeed, the other key event, which prompted this story, was the appointment of the first Muslim Adviser in the Prison Service primarily due to the failure to provide an environment which was free of institutional racism. So, an attempt at challenging cultural incompetence, a positive intervention for change, in prisons is presented as the sign of an impending moral panic about young violent Asian men who are prone to sex and drug crime. Attempts to rouse public concern over this issue are not new (Law, 1996). Lustgarten (1992), in his appraisal of the prospects for racial inequality and public policy in the 1990s, warns that the first goal for an agenda concerned with racial equality must be avoiding what in the worst case could be the

> British nightmare of the 1990s – one in which we go down the American road of virtually equating ethnic minorities with an unemployed or poor economic underclass stigmatised with mass criminality, coupled with the growing isolation, partially self-imposed, of a Pakistani Muslim community. (Lustgarten, 1992: 464)

The transference of American notions of a black underclass onto British Asians was sensationally presented in a recent Panorama programme (UNDERCLASS IN PURDAH, 29 March 1993). This was filmed in Bradford and showed Pakistani Muslims taking over drugs syndicates from Afro-Caribbeans, rejecting education and being in the process of forming a new section of the 'underclass'. The use of a recent analysis of the Labour Force Survey (Jones 1993) was used to set up an analysis of the economic and educational disadvantage of Muslims. This broad description was then entirely misrepresented as 'expert' support for an explanation of this pattern by reference to involvement in drugs, crime and violence, and attitudes to education and marital breakdown. This coded racism reworked a repertoire of images to do with prostitutes, drug-pushers and pimps and linked them to the 'uncivilised' behaviour of the whole Muslim community. The representation of Asian families displays an intriguing circuit of contradictory and ambivalent images from which the construction of 'new' forms of racist discourse can draw. They are presented as 'uncivilised' and 'backward' in their domination of women, dress, religious 'fundamentalism' and practices of ritual animal slaughter. They are presented as too 'modern' in their eagerness to create wealth and become self-employed, and by their takeover of the corner shop and English 'family values'. They are also presented as too 'post-modern' in their mobile, diasporic disruption of Britain's 'traditional culture' (Rattansi, 1994). To this we can now add the 'nightmare' of the Muslim underclass. Alibhai-Brown (1998) criticises the way in which Asian and black journalists 'increasingly put across crude and lurid accounts of black and Asian life'. The Panorama programme discussed above was made by an all-Asian team and during the process of responding to complaints about the programme the BBC claimed credibility due precisely to this fact. In a self-critical piece, Peregrine Worsthorne acknowledged his columns, written over 35 years in the *Sunday Telegraph*, on the subject of West Indian immigrants as being 'shameful'. He is not so repentant, however, on the subject of Muslim Asians who 'present a problem' because they fail to assimilate:

> they believe too much in family values rather than too little; take religion too seriously rather than not seriously enough and insist on defying the new mores of the permissive society rather than caving in to them. (*Guardian* 18 January 1997)

A further example of press reporting which sustains racist views, which used front-page pictorial images of black offenders and which used the same headline as the *Daily Mail* piece noted above has been singled out for criticism by Cottle (1999). FACES OF EVIL (*Bristol Evening Post*, 17 April 1996) showed 16 police 'mug shots' of black convicted drug dealers. Cottle's attack on this piece is a plea for greater truth and contextual depth. He argues that accuracy in the portrayal of the wider 'conditions of existence' of Bristol's black communities and contextual discussion of the rise of drug dealing are required in order to avoid perpetuating racist ideas. He also questions whether white drug dealers would have been treated similarly, whether the sensationalism of the headline fitted the two to four-year sentences, and the access to and use of police 'mug shots' to demonise and criminalise.

Another recent study of reporting in the local press by Ross (1998) also highlights the significance of race/crime linkages. This study examined reporting in the *Birmingham Evening Mail*, the *Coventry Evening Telegraph* and the *Wolverhampton Express and Star* using Critcher *et al.* (1975) who examined the period 1963–70 and Ross's own analysis of output from 12–18 May 1997 (just after the General Election). In the early period crime was the key theme with 22 per cent of items in 1963–70 being in this category. Crime dropped to 9 per cent in the short 1997 study, being overtaken by sports (43%) and entertainment (11%). Ross's main findings are that over time negative reporting, particularly on immigration, was much less in evidence but also that the range of stories and repertoire of images was much narrower. This journalistic trend is seen as rendering racism invisible and marginalising black participation in local community life. This invisibility did not extend to race and rape. Ross attacks the perpetuation of the 'black-as-criminal' stereotype by referring to a story concerning the gang-rape of two teenage girls. The ethnicity of the rapists was shown through pictures of the young black gang-members in several articles (1989: 239). This was not, however, referred to in the text indicating (hopefully) greater sensitivity in journalistic practice. The lack of reference to racist motives would indicate the lack of relevance of reporting the ethnic origin of the offenders.

These issues received wider public debate in November 1998. This surrounded the broadcasting of a *Dispatches* documentary on Channel 4 (19 November 1998) which highlighted the involvement of young black boys in cases of gang-rape. This programme opened with the assertion that gang sex attacks were happening 'more and more', and that 'most of the boys' involved were black. The first case presented involved a white girl who was attacked by a group of four black boys aged 14 to 15. In itself this case raised a set of serious issues relating to parental responsibilities, the role of law and children and sexuality. The justification for making the linkage between 'race' and rape was, however, made by reference to a wider context. Deborah Davies, the reporter responsible presented her team's research carried out over a three-month period, in the absence of official statistics. Fourteen cases of gang-rape that had come to court since 1996 were identified through discussion with criminal justice agencies. In these cases, it was said, 80 per cent of those accused were black and 65 per cent of the victims. All of the 14 cases involved black teenagers and in nine of the cases all those involved were black. In addition, half of the cases were found to have occurred in and around Brixton. In making explicit her intentions Davies said, in a televised debate about the programme later that evening, that the initial focus was children and sex and that it was only a 'long way down the production period' that it was realised that the majority of those involved were black. In addition, the presentation of context in the programme through giving a voice to black experts/ academics was sought by the production team, who approached 20 such individuals, all of whom declined to be interviewed. Nevertheless, drawing on these informal discussions the significance of racism in British society was acknowledged to be an important factor, as many of these young black boys were seen to be alienated by a 'white world with no chance of conventional success', hence they 'create their own'. Black youth workers from Brixton and a black head teacher gave their views. The latter reported finding at his school that in one group of 'ghastly boys', none older than 12, all carried condoms, and a black youth worker reported that such boys were 'not frightened of doing anything'. The drawing back from the focus on black youth alone was made towards the end of the programme when, in summing up, Davies said that, 'a section of young people white and black' needed to change their behaviour.

The programme was followed by a televised debate chaired by Darcus Howe and involving Davies, Lee Parker, the black youth worker who appeared on the programme, and a group of black professionals, which included a representative of the CRE. In an article which preceded the programme, Darcus Howe set out his position (TAKING ON THE TABOO, *Guardian*, 16 November 1998). His view was that the programme needed to be made, we needed to know and engage in the ensuing debate; 'Broadcast and be damned'. Interestingly he presents his own account of the causes and significance of black sexuality. The 'troubled sexuality' amongst blacks is seen to result from the 'licentiousness' of plantation society in the Caribbean and the cultural expectation of expressive sexuality with which young children are 'baptised at an early age'. This attempt to directly engage with the nature and meaning of black sexuality was, however, never made explicit in the programme, we were told there was something significant here and language, behaviour and brutal cruelty were described. Howe accepted that gang-rape is now mainly 'a black thing' and describes the programme as responding 'admirably to the challenge'. These views dictated the structure of the debate which was shown.

In direct opposition to this view, the *New Nation* (Britain's Number One Black Newspaper) described the programme as 'one of the most odious programmes ever to have appeared on television'. Two further articles appeared in the *Guardian* on the day the programme was broadcast. Davies presented her account in an article ANYONE HERE BEEN RAPED BY WHITE BOYS? (*Guardian*, 19 November 1998). She says, despite the 'unpalatable, politically incorrect' nature of the programme it was not scrapped because of the 'deep concern' of many black teachers, social workers and youth workers, and, she said, unless attitudes can be changed we are going to be 'locking up our children' and 'young lives, boys and girls, will be wrecked'. This piece was printed next to a shorter article by Raekha Prasad, WHAT BLACK VIEWERS THINK. She highlighted that the programme would further demonise black men as potential rapists but was particularly concerned to state the impact on black women. The Black Women's Rape Action Project demanded the programme's withdrawal as it was seen likely to lead to a decline in the reporting of rape by young black women through encouraging divided loyalties, and also increased concerns over institutional racism particularly among the police.

The Dispatches debate brought a number of positions into sharp relief. Chris Boardman, from the CRE, and Tony Sewell, a black academic whose recent work has dealt with young black masculinity (1997), presented consistent criticism of the programme stressing the lack of responsibility on the part of the programme-makers and the programme's spurious statistical inference:

> Yes – another stereotype has been created, we've got black muggers, we've now got black gang-bangers. If you're a young black man on the street you are now a potential gang banger...What's not right is to label a whole community based on the acts of individuals. (Boardman)

The statistical inference that most gang-rapists are black based on a small number of cases was criticised as 'dangerous', particularly in its presumed audience effects on the reproduction of racism. In pressing the question 'has this programme damaged the black community?', Howe elicited the response from Sewell that it had not done so as there had already been so many 'attacks, lies and dangerous stereotypes' on and about black young men. The lack of general information on child-on-child abuse and the lack of context were also challenged. In contrast, Lee Parker, the Brixton youth worker, felt the programme to be 'fair-handed', although the figures were 'painful' for the black community to hear, a community which was felt to be 'in denial'. The predominant view amongst the other participants was that there was a real and serious issue here that needed confronting and which required action other than criticism of the programme that had instigated the debate.

In seeking to identify whether and where racism lies in this programme it is useful to disaggregate questions of producer intentions, programme content and audience effects. The programme-makers' intentions encompassed a range of concerns; 'fitting' the controversial remit of the *Dispatches* series of documentaries, examining sexual activity amongst youngsters, exposing cases of child-on-child rape, giving voice to black practitioners and academics and encouraging wider debate. So, here there was expressed denial that racism was a factor in producer intentions, although the controversial linkage of race and sexuality was seen as valuable and significant in production terms. There was also evidence that anti-racism/black inclusion was a key production value and 'official' white voices from criminal justice agencies who were extensively listened to in the research for the programme were markedly absent. The programme content signified race explicitly through verbal references to black people and visual images of black boys and girls and 'concerned' black professionals. All black young boys were seen to be subject to alienation in a 'white world' and to be more likely to commit rape than white boys; in this sense race was negatively attributed. So, referring back to the discussion of conceptualisation in Chapter 1, irrespective of intentions, the programme content can be objectively defined as racist. But do racist images have racist effects on the audience? In the debate Sewell explicitly referred to the racist effect this programme would have on 'Joe Public' (even though the programme was seen as not doing damage to the black community). Howe replied that he (Sewell) was happy to stereotype white people at the same time as criticising the stereotyping of black people. This was a pertinent point and implies, as the debate showed, that the same set of text and images and examples of racism can have very different effects; prompting the expression of 'anti-racist' statements, contributing to the confronting of real social problems as well as contributing to the cultural reservoir of racist ideas. In other words, there is no necessary connection between racist content of a media item and the reproduction of racist ideas. This does not, however, undermine criticism of objective racism in the media and the importance of professional competence, organisational responsibility and regulation of media output.

Race and rape in US news

The Reverend Jesse Jackson, in comments made on a television panel, pointedly criticised the frequent linkages between black men and sexual controversy in American news (Dennis and Pease, 1997).

Cases such as the sexual harassment allegations against Justice Clarence Thomas, child sexual abuse charges against Michael Jackson and the rape conviction of boxer Mike Tyson were used to illustrate the sensational depth and high news values given to such stories. Two studies of media coverage of violence against women in the USA further illustrate serious issues in production, representation and consumption of 'race'-related news. The first study focuses on local news on television and in the press in Atlanta, Georgia (Meyers, 1997). As Meyers argues, local news tends to give more space to common, ordinary non-celebrity violence against women, in comparison to national network news where coverage tends to be limited to sensational or celebrity cases, such as the trial of Mike Tyson discussed below. This local study found that violence against African-American women was less likely to receive news coverage than violence against white wealthy women, and further that those African-American women who were represented in news items were more likely to be blamed as victims than white women (1997: 66). This relative invisibility of African-American women is indicative of a wider 'myth of invisibility' where there is less coverage of minority ethnic issues and communities in news generally which is seen as resulting particularly from the whitecentrism of newsroom decisions (Johnson and Sears, 1971; Pease, 1989; Campbell, 1995). In addition, Meyers argues that news coverage of violence against African-American women also reinforces stereotypes about them, and about African-American men and their propensity for involvement in violence, drug abuse and prostitution. Drawing on specific cases, she highlights the representation of fathers as prone to violence and sexual excess and mothers as inadequate, drug dealing and criminal. The focus on African-American female survivors of violence as drug and alcohol users and their involvement in prostitution are seen as contributing to their representation as being responsible for the violence against them (1997: 119–20). Although firmly situated within the stereotypes-and-distortions tradition of media content analysis with all its constraints and problems, Meyers shows that, despite the unevenness of coverage, such cases of violence increasingly feature on the news. They do, however, fail to depart from the 'grammar of race' (Hall, 1981). But, the extent to which a case of race-related rape is seen by news producers as more unusual, interesting or controversial and hence worthy of coverage because of its racial content is challenged by this research. The evidence of relative invisibility indicates the opposite position, with less attention being given to coverage of violence against African-American women.

The case of Mike Tyson and Desiree Washington was, in contrast, one of the most 'prominent, perhaps notorious, news stories' in 1992, in the USA (Lule, 1997). This provided an opportunity to examine in detail extensive news representation of race and rape. In 1992 former heavywight boxing champion Mike Tyson was accused and subsequently sentenced to six years imprisonment for the rape of Desiree Washington, a contestant in a Miss Black America beauty pageant. Lule (1997) has carried out an analysis of five major newspapers' reporting of this case over a nine-month period (July 1991–April 1992) which consisted of more than 500 stories. Lule argues that the reporting was 'flawed by its reliance upon racist imagery'. Tyson was cast in two ways in the reports; the black savage, inhuman, violent, sex-obsessed beast, or as the victim of social circumstance, including racism, who finally faltered (1997: 382). But Lule acknowledges two further key features of news coverage; there was no explicitly bigoted racist rhetoric employed and, secondly, the complexity of issues of gender and class which intertwined with representations of race. As with the case of Judge Clarence Thomas who was accused of sexual harassment by a former black junior colleague, Anita Hill (see Hall, 1992), identities became fragmented. In this case, a vocal section of the black community was reported as siding with Tyson, the black male, and against the 'bitch who set me up', a black female. Nevertheless, Lule affirms his view that news reporting reproduced 'modern racist symbolic types'. He refers here to modern racism as encompassing a position which takes the view that racial discrimination no longer exists and that problems facing the black community can be attributed to individual faults.

Interestingly, Lule accepts that members of the press are not overtly racist and are concerned to challenge the 'covert expression of racist stereotypes' and the language of news. In examining news language, Fowler argues that stereotypes are 'socially-constructed mental pigeon-holes into which events and individuals can be sorted' (1991: 17), and that they are a key creative feature of news which embody 'homocentric' news values (a preoccupation with nations and people like oneself and with defining those who are unlike as alien or threatening). Criticism of Lule's analysis, following Hall's discussion of the Thomas/Hill case, could be made in that he contributes to reducing the complexity of issues, positions and identities at stake in news reports to the two major stereotypes he identifies; squeezing content evaluation into two badly fitting categories. In replying to this criticism in a wider context, Fowler (1991: 232) emphasises the power of news discourse in that it 'constructs' readers/viewers/listeners as they must switch on to 'paradigms and stereotypes' presented to them, even if they are operating critically, in order to understand the meaning and signification embodied in those news items. The extent to which such construction of news is biased, predisposed or prejudiced in relation to issues of race and ethnicity is then of key importance.

Immigration

Coverage of migration has probably been the most consistently criticised sphere of news presentation relating to minority ethnic groups; for example Philo and Beatie (1999: 181) state that television news has presented a predominantly negative perspective on the migration process. In the USA, the most common news stereotype about migration is that immigration policy is 'out of control', with an overwhelming focus on the uncontrolled movement of illegal immigrants from Mexico. This is seen as a result of 'sloppy journalism [which] turns a complex and encouraging reality into a simplistic and ominous fiction' (Miller, 1997: 27). Samuleson, a *Newsweek* journalist, wrote that THE UNITED STATES CANNOT BE A SPONGE FOR MEXICO'S POOR (24 July 2000). He argued that 'our interest' [the American public] lies in less immigration, particularly because 'many Mexicans have little desire to join the American mainstream' and also because this 'would hurt those already here' through depression of wages, increased anti-Hispanic racism and the overwhelming of schools and social services. For Samuelson, the economic benefits of immigration are seen to be 'transcended' by the concern for national unity. This position echoes some of the campaign radio and television adverts used by right-wing Presidential candidate Pat Buchanan in the recent election in November 2000. Here, the overwhelming of English language by the numerous languages spoken by migrant groups was portrayed as undermining American society and causing too much disruption, for example in schools.

   In reporting on the key issues for the American electorate, *Newsweek* (6 November 2000: 37) explicitly focused on the failure of Bush and Gore to address the immigration question during the Presidential

Election campaign and asked them to address a 'central issue: how many immigrants are too many?' In calling for a return to the 'numbers game', *Newsweek* effectively demands that both Democrats and Republicans should 'play the race card'. This article portrays immigration as 'politically explosive', warning that 'whoever is elected won't be able to duck it for long'. The abandoning of the race card was a distinct feature of Bush's presidential campaign; ignoring immigration policy, steering clear of racially-coded appeals and presenting himself as a supporter of 'affirmative access' (if not fully fledged affirmative action) and tougher hate-crime legislation in the televised presidential debates. Cohn, writing in *New Republic* (13 Nov 2000) WHY THE REPUBLICANS ABANDONED THE RACE CARD, analysed the increasing failure of the Republican political line that the Democrats had caved in to black militancy through increasing federal spending on welfare, hence taxing middle-class white suburbanites to subsidise inner-city blacks. Increased Democratic emphasis on welfare reform, crime reduction and balanced budgets made this line less potent, hence the new Republican show of embracing anti-racism and diversity is seen as a roundabout way to appeal to moderate whites particularly women. The 2000 US election therefore strongly parallels the 1997 UK election with a strategic view that turning away from the 'old' rhetoric about race and immigration was vital to electoral success.

Strong criticism of immigration coverage has been made in relation to UK news. Philo and Beattie used a thematic analysis of BBC, ITN and Channel 4 news bulletins during the period 11–20 February 1995. News coverage during this period developed from the resignation of Charles Wardle, a junior Trade Minister, over the prospect of (in his own words) 'an unchecked flow of vast numbers of people who would possibly stay here and incur a huge cost for social security, housing and education, health and so on' (BBC1, 12 February 1997). This was seen as arising from a dismantling of border controls within the European Union. A key criticism made of news journalists was the lack of challenge or criticism of both these views and the terms of the debate, and a failure to use alternative information. Interestingly, such an alternative account was identified in the *Daily Telegraph* (20 February 1997) which commented that 'the reality of the migrant flow is that people are leaving Britain to work in these [EU] countries' (1999: 182). 'Alarmist' television news is accused of 'swallowing' an 'artificial scare story' dismissed by many experts and other newspaper journalists. Philo and Beattie identify 124 negative references to migrants, 115 references to the threat to Britain's border controls, and only 34 references to the plight of refugees and ethnic minorities and criticisms of the 'flood theory'. Migrant flows are also depicted in a highly selective racialised fashion with predominant visual and textual references to Third World and North African migrants. The silence of migrants' voices and their points of view is also criticised. Comments from organisations representing migrants, such as the JCWI, are seen as 'disparate fragments', unacknowledged and unexplored by journalists, which fail to alter the flow or terms of the debate.

The role of political leadership is seen as crucial here with government ministers talking of 'tides', 'floods' and 'swamping'. In addition, the IPPR's analysis highlights the crucial role played by Home Office press releases in shaping news agendas between 1994 and 1996 (Alibhai-Brown 1999). Here, study of 24 press releases showed a concentration on issues of illegal migration and 'bogus' refugees, the need for vigilance and control measures and also the welfare burden imposed by migrants. Particular criticism of the emotive use of words and phrases such as 'bogus', 'fraudsters' and 'milking the system' are also made (1999: 79). An inside Home Office source also reported that such releases were often made to 'win over papers like the *Daily Mail* and the *Express*'. These views are then seen as being uncritically promoted creating a conducive supportive climate during the reading of the Immigration and Asylum Bill in 1995. This indicates, therefore, xenophobic and racist political accounts being replayed and elaborated by news organisations.

The reproduction of racist ideas in this way also illustrates the fundamental importance of developing and sustaining both anti-racist political leadership and creative critical journalism. Gabriel (1998) goes further, emphasising that news coverage of migration promotes 'a sense of whiteness' in the private sphere. His analysis focused on press coverage in 1995/96 as the Immigration and Asylum Bill progressed through parliament. This covered the period just after Philo and Beattie's research (February 1995) and just before the news study reported on in Chapter 2 (November 1996 to May 1997). Gabriel emphasises that key drivers of Conservative policy were the perception that the bill would be a vote-winner in comparison to 'soft' Labour policy, and that rhetoric about British control in the face of EU 'lack' of control would appease Euro-sceptics. The *Daily Mail*, the *Daily Express* and the *Sun* are identified as supporting the Bill and elaborating 'coded whiteness' through references to linkages between migration, crime and terrorism. The broadsheets, including previous Conservative supporters such as *The Times*, *The Economist* and, less so, the *Daily Telegraph*, are identified as opposing the Bill. The strength of competing accounts and positions in the press and the 'diversity of white interests at stake' is in marked contrast to television coverage noted above. Analysis of the *Sun* (21 November 1996) showed concern for both the interests of (white) taxpayers – through calls for reductions in benefit payments to migrants; (white) consumers – through acknowledgement of the contribution of immigrant labour to economic production; and (white) employers – through claims that migrant labour was being used to hold down pay and conditions.

Local radio was found to be ambivalent and more balanced in news coverage of migration, but also much more open to giving voice to spokespeople from the National Campaign Against Immigration and Asylum. Television and the press are criticised for their overall silence in covering demonstrations, pickets and other actions taken by opposition campaigning groups, with the exception of 'human interest' stories of some individual refugees who were facing deportation. Such silences are seen by Gabriel as contributing to an 'under-whelming' level of press coverage in comparison to the attention given to immigration in the 1960s and 1970s due to a relative lack of interest in a 'battle-fatigued issue'. Similarly to Philo and Beattie, Gabriel stresses the power of news organisations to generate support for exclusionary versions of British identity and British legislation. These studies provide a valuable contribution to the task of unmasking racism in the news, despite limited and selective attention to news output.

Following the introduction of the Immigration and Asylum Act 1996, a number of key trends appear to have contributed to a changing pattern of news coverage. Decreasing confidence in, and support for, the Conservative Party by news organisations appears as a continuing trend through the General Election campaign in 1996/7, indicating the likelihood of reducing support for the 'old' party-line on immigrant numbers. Political leadership, from both parties, on race and migration was continuing to play a significant role in shaping news agendas. Here, 'strong' Labour rhetoric on the maintenance of immigration control and 'weak' Labour rhetoric on anti-racism ran parallel to 'strong' Conservative plays for the minority ethnic vote. The sleight-of-hand here with the switching of 'expected' party agendas led to the articulation of a high-profile consensus that the classic race and immigration card would not feature in the General Election debates, and that there was little political difference for journalists to exploit. These issues came to the fore in March 1997. (This also reflects the continued decline in public interest in immigration as an issue during General Election campaigns. Saggar (1992) notes that this issue did not feature in voters' top-ten concerns in the 1983 and 1987 elections.) Lastly, the concerted efforts of the coalition of campaigning organisations against immigration and asylum controls to secure a presence in the news, particularly for the voices of 'ordinary' protesters and refugees facing deportation, was beginning to reap some reward. The action taken by refugees on hunger strike in Rochester prison in January 1997 provided a valuable vehicle for presentation of campaigners' views in the news.

In examining dominant messages in news items it was shown in Chapter 2 that the pattern of reporting across news organisations tends to show some change compared to Philo and Beattie's account and confirms the trends identified in Gabriel's account. Radio, and to a lesser extent television news, were much more likely to carry items critical of immigration and asylum policy, arguing for an improvement in migrant rights and showing the plight of refugees. They also allowed greater space for campaigning organisations to be heard. The tabloids were the only news medium to persistently carry an unequivocally hostile set of messages about migration; arguing for stricter controls on immigration, reduction of the 'welfare burden' of migrants and clampdowns on their criminal activities. What is particularly interesting here is the pattern of interaction between political messages on race and migration and the pattern of hostile and sympathetic news coverage more generally. News items conveying both sorts of messages gradually escalated through the General Election campaign from November 1996 to March 1997 culminating in Nicholas Budgen's high-profile pressure for the 'old' Conservative line on immigrant control to be brought out of the closet (see below). However, after Major and Blair's joint statements refusing to make such a move and opposing the terms of this debate, hostile immigrant news items all but disappeared from general news coverage for the rest of the General Election period up to May. This did not reflect an overall loss of news interest in this issue, however, as pro-immigrant items focusing on the plight of refugees, for example, did not abate but continued to appear (see dates of immigration news headlines in Chapter 2). This may indicate the 'uncritical' approach of editors, producers and journalists in accepting the cross-front bench consensus on this issue and the central importance of political leadership in shaping race news agendas. It did not, however, reflect a dramatic change in news values and proved to be short-lived.

Hostile coverage, particularly of asylum-seekers, remains a persistent feature of news coverage. However, Alibhai-Brown (1999: 79) notes the 'remarkable shift' in Home Office press releases between the 1997 General Election and October 1998 with a focus now on the positive attributes of immigrants and multicultural Britain, less rhetoric and more constructive presentation of information. But, the theme of 'abuse' of immigration rules and asylum regulations although less pervasive still appeared as a regular theme, both in Home Office statements and, more emotively, in the press. In January 1999, press releases from the National Assembly Against Racism highlighted continuing problems in news coverage (NAAR, 12 January 1999, 25 January 1999). A range of national and local newspapers are criticised for pursuing inflammatory racist campaigns against asylum-seekers; blaming them for high crime rates and hospital closures and describing them as 'sewage', 'foreign predators' and 'migratory villains' who 'poison' and 'pollute'. A *Daily Mail* article SUBURBIA'S LITTLE SOMA-LIA claimed that Somalis are 'hostile, aggressive and suspicious' and 'antagonistic to any outsider', and it quotes immigration officials as saying that Somalis coming to Britain are not genuine refugees because they are not starving and have some money. This article prompted a demonstration outside the *Mail*'s offices. The weakness of the law on incitement to racial hatred, the inability of the Press Complaints Commission to act in these cases and the *Mail*'s argument that such reporting is not formally defined as racist provide the freedom for such news coverage to continue. Recent reporting of the speech by Ann Widdecombe, the Conservative Shadow Home Secretary, at the Conservative Party Conference in October 1999 in *The Times* (6 October) makes explicit reference to her pledge 'to halt the flood of asylum-seekers by reinstating the list of safe countries' (hence speeding up refusals) and for 'increasing the use of detention'.

In an article examining the *Daily Mail*'s coverage of refugee issues, Roy Greenslade charts a shift from coverage in 1998, which 'turned asylum-seeker into a swear word, a racist epithet as recognisably repugnant as nigger or Jew', to coverage in spring 1999. More generous sentiments were expressed in an article headlined WHY BRITAIN MUST OFFER SANCTUARY which urged the government to 'take its fair share' of Kosovan refugees (*Guardian*, 12 April 1999). Roy Greenslade acknowledged the 'tentative steps towards liberalism', but saw these to be driven by 'implacable opposition' to Labour Government policy, here he felt that the *Daily Mail*'s 'heart is in the right place. It just needs a head transplant'.

The speed of switching from generosity to hostility, and the fickle nature of migration reporting was evident in more recent coverage. One recent example of press hostility to the existing system of managing illegal migration, through a combination of weak government policy, a heavily constrained immigration service and easy access on cross-channel ferries, was a full front-page item; COME ON IN, MAIL INVESTIGATION REVEALS HOW SCANDALOUSLY SIMPLE IT IS FOR ILLEGAL MIGRANTS TO ENTER BRITAIN (*Daily Mail*, 27 November 1999). Here, the 'exploitable welfare state' becomes the real scandal and the 'Kosovans, Algerians, Albanians, Iraqis and Kurds' who make a 'beeline' for Britain are seen as 'just seeking a better life'.

A last, disturbingly titled piece that indicates the continuity of xenophobic reaction to migration in some parts of the news media was in the *Daily Telegraph* (INVASION OF 400,000 JOBSEEKERS FROM EU, 1 December 1999). Here, the most worrying feature is the use of the word 'invasion'. Why not use a more appropriate or welcoming headline? The headline fails to represent the article as it notes that 178 000 people left Britain over the same period, that 80 000 of the in-migrants were Britons returning from work abroad, and that there is urgent economic demand for labour that cannot be met within Britain. So, rather than 'invasion', reference could have been made to a 'Vital inflow of much needed labour' which would have given a more appropriate 'fit' with the content. Indeed this information drawn from various sources of migration data could have been used to disrupt the whole basis of refugee and asylum reporting. The article quotes there to have been 58 000 refugee and asylum-seekers arriving in 1998; in other words they make up just over 10 per cent of incoming migrants. Journalistic challenges here could then be to report on the remaining 90 per cent of diverse types of migrants, to highlight British economic needs and the benefits of migration and to present a more informed picture of the complexity of migration flows. However, the continued strength of political rhetoric about the need for 'strong' controls and a clampdown on illegal immigration still appears to dominate in many news stories.

Bias and prejudice

There are two relevant debates to be addressed in analysing questions of the shaping, distortion or blatant misrepresentation in news coverage. Firstly there is a range of competing debates which have sought to examine issues of bias in the news with no specific focus on 'race'-related issues (Gunter, 1997; Iyengar and Reeves, 1997). Secondly, there are a wide range of studies which have sought to examine questions of racial prejudice or racial bias with no specific focus on news media and communication issues (Sampson, 1999). In addition, this section will present new material on racial bias in television, radio and newspapers drawing on the study introduced in the previous chapter.

News journalism is a complex process involving the social construction of reality through a range of organisational and production techniques. Decisions about which stories to select, what priority to give them and how to present them, amongst others, involve principles of selection and value-laden assumptions. Bias of this sort is inherent and its impact on outcomes, for example different news agendas across media sources, was shown in Chapter 2. However, McQuail (1992) has argued that it is evidence of repetition and continuity that is required to identify bias; a 'consistent tendency' that shows deviation from objective truth. Hence, as Stevenson and Greene (1980) have identified, bias would involve 'systematic differential treatment' of a particular point of view over a period of time. This latter definition comes close to the concept of direct racial discrimination; less-favourable treatment of a particular racial or ethnic or national group in comparison to the way that other groups are normally treated. Measurement here hinges on the quantitative and qualitative indicators of 'treatment'.

In a thorough account of the measurement of news bias, Gunter (1997: 24) has usefully elaborated the range of factors that need to be taken into account which are; 'factualness', 'accuracy', 'completeness', 'truthfulness', 'balance', 'neutrality' and 'impartiality'. In assessing the truth of news presentation, factors such as the depth of information, checkability (of sources), readability, and range of topics and aspects of topics (completeness and gaps) can be assessed by measuring output and checking against audience memory and comprehension as well as other records of events, perceptions of those who provided information (sources) and eyewitness comparisons. In addition, assessment of news presentation involves consideration of visual devices (camera angles, shot framing etc.), headlines, sequencing, summaries and use of captions and pictures. In assessing news selection, factors such as contemporary significance to audiences (relevance and ordering/placement of items) can be examined in relation to external or professional criteria. Normative assessment of agendas held by audiences, institutions and political parties, interest groups and 'experts' can be compared to news coverage to assess relevance. Examination of professional criteria and practice in prioritisation and selection of news stories can also reveal those factors which influence selection including drama, surprise, proximity, sex, personalities and scandal (Hetherington, 1985). The question of balance in news selection can be examined through attention to quantitative 'stopwatch criterion'; for example time given to political parties and source bias, as well as qualitative forms of analysis including use of language, choice of words and phrasing, structuring of text and frames of meaning. These questions can also be assessed by reference to audience perceptions of impartiality and understanding of issues. All of these factors come together in Gunter's call for attention to the 'bias against proper understanding' (Jay and Birt, 1977) in the news.

In the measurement of prejudice there are a variety of forms and types of 'unjustified, usually negative attitudes' (Sampson, 1999) which need to be considered. Prejudice may be held in relation to a 'race', an ethnic group or a nation or part of a nation. Recent debates over the need for decentralised news coverage of Scotland and improved placement of Scottish news items has often revolved around perceptions of the nation and interpretations of the national interest. Here, the BBC is charged with serving the 'national interest' and has sought to use such an argument to defend itself against this claim. Hence prejudice in favour of the British nation is part of the news media's regulatory framework and often becomes explicit in times of war, for example during the Gulf War. Ethnocentrism refers to the 'application of the norms of one's own culture to that of others' (Brown, 1965: 183). This form of prejudice may underlie news values in media organisations that operate in the interests of one nation and one culture and may be found to be influencing issues of relevance in news selection or in establishing a regime of truth (Foucault, 1980: 131) in news presentation. Qualitative assessment of producer intentions may reveal such attitudes. Cottle's study of a group of BBC producers working in the Multicultural Programmes Department in the early 1990s highlighted

two aspects. Firstly, the producers' own commitment to enhance
representation of minority ethnic experiences and agendas on television was clear, but also their own experiences of a 'prevailing ethos
of programme conservatism' and an 'institutionalised and under-
ground racism, especially from technical staff' (1997: 63). A further
example of overtly racist journalism was highlighted in a 'confession'
by Peregrine Worsthorne printed in the *Guardian* (OUT OF SIGHT, INTO
HINDSIGHT, 18 January 1997); 'I wrote a lot of wicked nonsense' he
admitted referring to his pieces on 'coloured immigration' as 'shameful'.

Consideration was given to assessment of racial bias in the television
news by African-Caribbean and Asian viewers in Chapter 1. Here, over
a half of African-Caribbeans and over a third of Asians perceived
a general racial bias against blacks/ethnic minorities, with a much
lower proportion perceiving a racial bias in favour of whites on the
four main channels. On satellite and cable news, the level of perceived
racial bias against blacks/ethnic minorities was comparable, with
about 40 per cent of both groups identifying this disturbing trend.
This is indicative of a 'collective failure to provide an appropriate
service' to these communities on the part of news agencies. Bias
against blacks/ethnic minorities was felt to be evident through
the representation of white cultural values, partial reporting and
through the perpetuation of stereotypes such as the focus on black
crime:

> It's always about crime, about violence or about some rape someone's
> committed. Or a stabbing or loud music. (African-Caribbean viewer quoted
> in Mullan, 1996: 34)

A more specific form of bias assessment was carried out using data
drawn from the analysis of British news items during November 1996
to May 1997 (see Chapter 2). Other than the inevitable bias in selection
of news items, a more specific form of negative bias may occur in terms
of a deliberate shaping of items to show, present or promote hostility
to minority ethnic groups in the UK. Equally, items may show either a
bias in favour of minority groups or be broadly neutral in the treatment of news. Each item was assessed against these criteria. As Gunter
notes, these evaluative codes are generally a 'predictor of effect on
audience' rather than a measure of 'intention of the sender', but where,
as in this study, differential selection and presentation is evident across

news media then we have a clearer indication that we are highlighting the recurring patterns of editorial choice (1997: 26).

Using this analysis, 88 per cent of items were found to be neutral, 8 per cent were found to be biased in favour of ethnic minority groups, and only 4 per cent biased against. Perception of bias does need further research to assess the extent to which response to items differs across audiences and readers. Also, as noted in Chapter 2, reliability checks on coding of bias and all other categories were carried out.

No negatively-biased items were identified on television news, and about 9 per cent were felt to be in favour of ethnic minority groups. On radio, a similar proportion of positive bias (9%) to television was identified and only two negatively-biased items were identified. One of which on What the Papers Say on Radio 4's Today programme (15 April 1997) reproduced verbatim a *Daily Express* item which reported the 'scandal of welfare abuse' of a Brazilian immigrant who required £100 000 of medical treatment. This was further reported as 'penalising hard-working British citizens in order to support people who have no right to be here'. This item was selected for inclusion in the press review piece early in the programme and then omitted later on; why it was chosen for inclusion as a relevant and significant news item is unknown.

The bulk of biased items were found in the press (78%), and of these the majority were biased in favour of ethnic minority groups (70 items were positive and 47 negative). Positively-biased items were found predominantly in the *Guardian* and the *Independent* (together they contained 58% of these items), smaller numbers were found in every other newspaper. These items mainly fell into the categories of exposing racism, promoting the rights and needs of migrants and supporting action to improve the material conditions of minorities in Britain. Negatively-biased items were more evenly spread with most appearing in the *Sun* and the *Daily Telegraph* (together they accounted for 42% of these items) and, again, smaller numbers were found in every other newspaper. The main theme of these items was immigration. Four '*News of the World* Investigates' items:

WE CATCH 350 MIGRANTS IN WEDDING CON SCANDAL (18 January 1997),

CHEATING MIGRANTS GRAVE FIDDLE (30 March 1997),

DEAD MAN WALKING, HE RIPS OFF DSS FROM GRAVE (23 March 1997) and

DOLE FRAUDSTERS FERRY HOP TO A FORTUNE (11 May 1997),

all provided examples of cases of illegal immigrants fiddling welfare benefits. The reporting in these items was generally terse and factual, but they include pictures and references to Asian and African identities which make a clear link between 'race' and fraud.

Three items by former Conservative MP Nicholas Budgen on immigration led the 'play the race card' coverage. The *Independent* was cited as being responsible for instigating Nicholas Budgen's concern with Labour's immigration policy as he said 'It was not until I read it...that I thought this is something that needs investigating'. The *Independent* provided him with an opportunity to state his case after his second rebuke by John Major, HOW LONG SHALL WE AVOID THE IMMIGRATION ISSUE? (27 March 1997). Here he commented that 'private promises and the denial of debate can only encourage tension', such as, 'extra-parliamentary action in the shape of both National Front activity and riots'. In addition, he stresses that 'many West Midlanders feel themselves to be strangers in their own pubs, schools and streets', as, 'three constituencies here have ethnic minorities over 30%'. These views he denies amount to racism, 'I defend myself from accusations of racism', although he admits, 'I do not know what is meant by racist'. Budgen presents a political discourse which links 'lax immigration policy' with 'white indigenous resentment' and the 'British' feeling 'like strangers in their own land' and 'immigrant resentment against the whites' (*Daily Mail*, 13 March 1997). Attempts to 'liberalise and weaken the immigration laws' are therefore seen as being detrimental to 'race relations', 'ethnic communities' and the 'white community'. This constitutes a particular form of racist discourse as it refers to an essential white culture which finds its most important expression as a nation; naturalised expression of hostility to outsiders particularly Asians and West Indians; the construction of exclusive ethnically defined 'communities'; an absence of reference to racial hierarchy; and a related denial that this perspective is racist. These are the key elements of 'new' racism, or cultural racism that has been identified in Conservative Party discourse since the Second World War.

In two *Times* editorials, the first (QUESTIONS UNANSWERED, 9 December 1996) contained a negative linkage of 'rabid dogs and asylum seekers' in the context of criticism of government position on EU policy, and the second (RED CROSS BUNGLE, 19 December 1996) criticism of Red Cross food parcels for asylum seekers as an 'inefficient' and 'inappropriate response' to poverty and exclusion from benefits. An *Independent* item, BRITAIN IS 'HAVEN FOR TERRORISTS', (10 December 1996), linked terrorism and Islam in the UK through unbalanced reporting of comments from Charles Pasqua, French Interior Minister.

Apart from items relating to immigration and asylum-seekers, negative bias tended to be occasional, sporadic and varying in context. A rare example of anti anti-racism was found in the *Daily Mail*, HOW THE RACE ROW ZEALOTS PROMOTE RACISM (29 November 1996). This attacked the 'bleats of the multi-culturalists' and accused the CRE of seeking to 'undermine race relations', 'slipping into the territory of the thought police and Franz Kafka', having a 'victim-led mentality', 'meddling' and producing 'grotesque administrative obstacle courses'. A *Yorkshire Evening Post* editorial (IMPASSE CHOKES FRANCE, 26 November 1996) which in commenting on striking French lorry drivers, indulges in anti-French prejudice; 'Britain knows all too well that quaint Gallic tendency . . . to let someone braver and bolder take all the risks and spill their blood'. Ridiculing multiculturalism was evident in a variety of contexts including a front-page image of John Major in a turban (KHYBER ASS, *Mirror*, 14 January 1997) and an editorial about multicultural education (HISTORY TEACHING IS BUNK, *Daily Telegraph*, 8 January 1997). Letters columns contained much stereotypical invective, with examples including reference to the 'creeping Islamisation of Britain' (*Daily Mail*, 14 March 1997), although this was placed adjacent to a pro-Islam letter, and the failure of Africans to care about their heritage and artefacts (*Independent*, 25 February 1997).

A recent small-scale study of coverage of ethnic minorities and news in Northern Ireland by Fawcett (1998) draws on the 'older' notions of elite discourse which are seen to be producing a failure to recognise racism in Northern Ireland and marginalisation of ethnic minority concerns. Fawcett identifies a media consensus, which contains the following elements:

- racism is not a major problem in Northern Ireland – those responsible for racist attacks are deviants;
- white settler society is doing what it can to help ethnic minorities;
- Chinese and Indians are responsible citizens who contribute to the economy;
- Travellers are irresponsible;

- ethnic minorities are different, inferior and uncivilised; and
- ethnic minority concerns are not a part of the mainstream political agenda (1998: 112).

This is an ambivalent set of messages which are both inclusive and exclusive, and which also reflect the 'late' attention to ethnic minority issues in Northern Ireland and the much lower presence of ethnic minority journalists across newspapers and television compared to mainland Britain.

This study also sought to identify the key messages contained in news items, similar to the case study in Chapter 2. Overall, 45 items were examined covering the period March to May 1996, of which Fawcett found 31 to contain a 'strong element of negativity or bad news', or 69 per cent. This is a particularly worrying finding given the difference to trends at the national level, and the failure to show significant improvement. Crime is a persistent theme, and here Fawcett identifies the *Sunday Life* and the *Sunday World* as representing ethnic minorities, particularly Nigerians and Chinese, as criminals. One journalist, John Cassidy, confronted by Fawcett over an article entitled NIGERIANS IN CASH FIDDLE TARGET ULSTER (*Sunday Life*, 7 April 1996) agreed that he had implied that all Nigerians were criminals, but that this had not occurred to him at the time.

In relation to reporting on issues of racism in Northern Ireland, Tom Collins, the editor of the *Irish News*, acknowledged that 'the media has been complacent and lazy in many respects' (Fawcett, 1998: 117). This vacuum of editorial and journalistic responsibility was filled by the priorities of the mainstream political agenda, and this shows the significance of the role of political leadership in determining news. Here, the silence of the Conservative Government on ethnic minority issues was being simply reproduced, with only two press releases over the period June 1995 to May 1996 referring to these issues.

Given the 'passivity' of the media, this study also highlights the importance of news intervention by ethnic minority organisations themselves. Fawcett cites the example of the Northern Ireland Council for Travelling People who sought to push their concerns through seeking news coverage and achieved change in the 'parameters of public debate' which has increasingly 'accommodated their needs and concerns' (1998: 120). The legitimate concerns and dangers over increased news coverage, voiced by Traveller and Chinese organisations, were that they may reinforce stereotypes, for example of Travellers as trouble-makers, and damage relations between white customers and Chinese businesses. This final point was emphasised by a Chinese waiter who had been interviewed for a programme on racist attacks, and who had been told by other Chinese 'You shouldn't went on TV'. He strongly felt, however, that being abused was 'not something that you would live with, no way'. The focus on Chinese community issues is of particular interest here as these generally receive very little coverage in the British news.

Naming racial and ethnic groups

The ways in which particular groups of people are categorised and referred to in the news are of vital significance; they provide a set of conceptual tools with which to construct an understanding of how the world works. Referring to racial groups can easily give the impression that races are real (Law, 1996). Social Darwinism, physical anthropology, eugenics, social ecology and socio-biology have used racial categories and attempted to elaborate a physical or biological basis for social and cultural difference. These ideas influenced the development of sociological approaches from the 1920s onwards with the analysis of races as *cultural groups*, with a focus on processes of adaptation, assimilation and integration (Park and Burgess, 1921; Park, 1950). Races were, therefore, real things which came into conflict with each other, interacted and, hence, these processes became an object of study as '*race relations*'. Miles (1984, 1993), Goldberg (1993) and Guillaumin (1995) have consistently argued against the use of the race idea in social analysis as it is seen to necessarily suggest that certain social relationships are natural and inevitable. The belief or implicit suggestion that races are real is therefore treated with the utmost suspicion, race is seen to be essentially ideological and the analytical task is to explain why social relationships are interpreted in this way. The concept of racialisation, which was first developed by Fanon (1967) and subsequently elaborated by Miles (1989) refers to a dynamic process, an extension or resurgence of racist statements and related behaviour where race is used to perceive and define boundaries between groups of people. This process can be seen in British news media and parliamentary discourse where debates from the early 1900s onwards over immigration policy showed such characteristics. The continued use of the race idea is seen as reinforcing dominant common-sense ideas that different races exist and have a biological reality. A startling globally publicised example of this was to be found at the opening ceremony of the football World Cup in France in 1998. *The Times* front page carried a picture of the opening parade through Paris showing a 38–ton yellow giant who represented the 'yellow' race. The accompanying article entitled A GALLIC FESTIVAL OF HOOPLA, ART . . . AND FOOTBALL stated that:

> From the four corners of Paris, the plastic giants representing races from four continents, shuffled at precisely 1mph on feet made from forklift trucks. (*The Times*, 10 June 1998)

The difficulties and dilemmas of moving beyond such obvious and normal 'race-thinking' and moving on to envision a 'colour-blind future' have been discussed by Williams in the 1997 Reith lectures. Here, she states that:

> It is a tribute to the power of television, perhaps, that the very tiny minority of black and Asian people in Great Britain . . . is the focus of such immense anxiety. (Williams, 1997: 27)

Van Dijk's study of news terminology referring to minorities in the mid-1980s confirmed that the British press reported ethnic relations using racial categories; 'ethnic' references were rarely used, 'immigrant' was much less frequent and specific nationality references were rare (1991: 55). In contrast, the Dutch press tended to use specific names for minority groups such as 'Moroccans' or 'Surinamese'.

In the case study of news items in 1996/97, simple racial references were still the most commonly-used terms across all media in the items analysed. References to 'blacks' were found in over 25 per cent of items and to 'whites' in over 12 per cent of items. There was little significant difference in usage across media sources. 'Afro-Caribbean' was rarely used (1.5%), and, when it is, it is much more likely to be found in broadsheets than any other media type. 'West Indian' was used even less and 'coloured' hardly at all. 'Asian' was in common usage (8%) particularly on television and in the broadsheets. Religious reference within this category was less common with Muslims, Hindus and Sikhs being specified in 4.8 per cent of items and usage more common in the broadsheets. This reflects the general tendency to think and report about minority groups in racial terms despite differing perceptions of groups themselves. Specific reference to national identity, that is Indian, Pakistani and Bangladeshi, was more rare (2.2%). Chinese and Hong Kong Chinese references were also rare (0.5%) reflecting the lack of news coverage given to these groups in the British context. The most common general group term was 'minorities' (5.1%) which was again more likely to be found in the broadsheets. Reference to 'immigrants' (3.1%) was evident, whereas 'foreigners' was relatively rare (0.4%), and these terms were usually found in the tabloids. Specific usage of national identities was more common on radio.

Despite the persistence of racial references, in contrast to the mid-1980s ethnicity is being increasingly given precedence in news discourse. Ethnic is now being used frequently in the press (*Guardian* and *Mail*) to refer to black groups and/or black minority ethnic groups – for example the ethnic vote, ethnic communities, ethnic party. 'Ethnic' has acquired a racialised coding and has replaced black in many instances. This is a poor use of language and should be criticised as we all have an ethnicity; it normalises white ethnicities and this coding acts to reproduce racist ideas.

The recognition of hybrid, mixed forms of ethnicity has yet to show in news coverage, as only 0.5 per cent of items reflected this dynamic in naming groups and individuals. Use of terminology remains problematic and dynamic, as exemplified by a number of news items concerning the racial and ethnic identity of the golfer, Tiger Woods, who refused attempts at racial categorisation and claimed a Cabilinaisian mixed identity. This topic was broached in the *Guardian* (22 May 1997) as its G2 section ran with a front page entitled BEIGE BRITAIN with photographs of 35 facially-different people. The subtitle contained an interesting gaffe. It said, 'A new race is growing up. It's not black, it's not white and it's not officially recognised. Welcome to the mixed-race future'. Here, an attempt to talk up ethnic and cultural hybridity and the increasing irrelevance of mono-dimensional forms of official categorisation is couched in racial terms. A real 'new race'? Surely this does nothing more than reinforce the Britishcentric view and belief that races are in fact a biological reality.

In comparison to analysis of terms used in UK news coverage a decade ago, significant change has been observed. There is less use of racial categories although they still have a high profile. There is also increased use of specific references to ethnicity and nationality although problems and difficulties in usage remain.

In the USA, *Newsweek* produced a special edition on 'Redefining Race in America' together with a live conference in Birmingham, Alabama. *Newsweek* has a tradition of producing such special race reports over the last thirty years including editions which have focused on civil rights programmes, the role of black men, affirmative action, the Los Angeles riots and O.J. Simpson. Entman and Rojecki (2000) were highly critical of the edition on affirmative action (3 April 1995) entitled 'Race and Rage', which they argue heightened racial animosity through framing the issue as one of irreconcilable difference of interest between black beneficiaries and white 'losers'. The issue of affirmative action coverage is examined further in Chapter 5. However, they also acknowledge that coverage addressed the complexity of affirmative action programmes, gave useful case studies of programmes and gave space to William Julius Wilson and a black *Newsweek* Editor, Ellis Cose, who argued in favour of such action. Five years on, with a realisation that attacking affirmative action had not generated white votes in the 1996 Presidential Election and that a majority of the American public continued to support affirmative action, as with immigration, had receded as a key political battleground. Instead, both the political and *Newsweek* message changed to one of emphasising ethnic diversity:

> every day, in every corner of America, we are redrawing the colour lines and redefining what race really means. It's not just a matter of black and white anymore: the nuances of brown, yellow and red mean more – and less – than ever. (THE NEW FACE OF RACE, *Newsweek*, 18 September 2000)

So, white-black divisions are now referred to as 'ancient' history, yet new divisions are still being presented in racial terms – red, yellow and brown. These precise terms were picked up on and used by Bush in one of the televised Presidential debates in October 2000 and are likely to be continually repeated in the news and by the public. Hispanic immigration, increasing intermarriage across ethnic groups, the reduction of white Californians to a numerical minority in their state, a total of three states and the capital city having a non-white majority, the coming emergence of Latinos as the nation's largest majority by 2010, and of course the 'new' popularity of stars such as Jennifer Lopez and Ricky Martin are seen as changing the face of America. However, we also see a brief nod to the 'old' divisions in this piece which recognises the 'suffering from poverty, imprisonment and racial profiling' disproportionately born by African-Americans. But this is brushed aside in the new world where now it is 'suddenly cool to be mixed'.

Here, the talking up of ethnic and cultural hybridity is also implicitly presented in racial terms. *Newsweek*'s 'America 2000: a Map of the Mix' presents a picture of the population of each state as either white, black, Hispanic, Asian and Pacific Islander and American Indian/ Eskimo/Aleutian Islander, we have no 'mixed' category here. A further item which discusses the 'flood' of Hispanic immigrants into south and midwest America is entitled BROWN AGAINST BROWN. Why is it that racial terms are emphasised in this way? We are told that 'scores of towns have *browned* virtually overnight' (emphasis added). The article provides anti-racist reporting, exposing hostility from 'white old-timers', who made comments such as 'the s.o.b.s live like riffraff', criticising rising crime, chickens in the yard and 'yakking' in Spanish, as well as hostility from long-established Mexican-Americans (Chicanos) to the newcomers. One recent migrant, Perez, is reported as saying Chicanos may be my race (*raza*) but not my people (*gente*), resenting their hostility and displaying the taken-for-granted nature of race-thinking which is equally reflected in news reports.

Conclusion

The persistence of racist messages in the news media and the shape these messages have taken has been the focus of this chapter. Renewed linkage of race and rape is a particularly worrying aspect of contemporary media coverage. In examining the debate over a Dispatches programme it was found that producer and journalistic intentions contained an ambivalent mix of racism and anti-racism; with explicit desire to promote negative linkages between race and sexuality combined with a concern to give voice to black professionals. The programme content was more obviously racist in presenting black young boys as more likely to commit rape than white boys, with a lack of convincing evidence. The programme's effects were also seen as ambivalent; prompting the expression of anti-racist statements, contributing to the confronting of real social problems as well as contributing to the cultural reservoir of racist ideas. By way of contrast, Owen's account of the Channel 4 documentary, The Stephen Lawrence Story, highlights the space available for 'impassioned and political' documentary film-making about racial injustice in the British media (Owens, 1999).

The American evidence showed how issues of race continue to influence and structure reporting of rape cases. The relative invisibility of violence against African-American women in news coverage was combined with the presentation of a repeated range of stereotypical images; savage, violent, sexually-excessive black fathers, drug-abusing criminal mothers and inadequate victims. In a wider review of American news it was found that African-Americans were generally portrayed as 'rap stars, drug addicts or welfare mothers', Latinos were portrayed as 'aliens and foreigners', Asian-Americans as 'inscrutable, manipulative' invaders of US business, and Native Americans as 'Indian drunks' (CIIJ, 1994). These stereotypes were seen as exemplifying whitecentric newsroom decisions and homocentric news values (a preoccupation with nations and people like oneself and with defining those who are unlike as alien or threatening) (Aldrich, 1999).

Reporting on migration issues continues to be a source of racial hostility. This has been frequently led by government sources with concern expressed over abuse, fraud and deceit and other forms of illegal activity. News coverage of this issue has been shown to be often characterised by poor sloppy journalism with little attention to the real costs and benefits of complex migration flows. Overall, the crucial 'steering' role of the major political parties and, in particular, government leadership on these issues has been established as central to the rise and fall of media hostility to racialised migrant groups.

The assessment of bias in news reporting was found to be a complex affair involving a range of strategies to evaluate news presentation, selection, balance and impartiality (Gunter, 1997). Editorial bias in selection of race items was indicated in Chapter 2 by the identification of differing news agendas across different news media. An evaluation of more deliberate racial bias in British news content confirmed the evidence of significant progress and improvement in reporting race issues in the news media in comparison to the 1980s. Overall, most items were found to be neutral with more evidence that journalists were prepared to advocate on behalf of minorities than express deliberate hostility towards them. In Northern Ireland, a study of newspapers showed that these encouraging trends were not in evidence. Minority ethnic groups' concerns were largely marginalised in the news reflecting weak political leadership, poor journalistic professionalism and unconscious racism.

Labels and names for particular groups carry particular and changing ideological baggage. Use of categories and terminology requires sensitivity to the people concerned. The British news media operates in a confused position retaining often spurious racial categories and using ethnicity with little understanding. Black people are still twice as likely to be racially described than white people in news items, and in many cases this is unnecessary. Overall, race-thinking pervades news coverage of migrants and ethnic relations and the thoroughly mistaken notion that races are real is continually reinforced.

Bashing, exposing and criticising the racial bias in news journalism and media representation remains an important strategy for change. This approach developed organisational momentum in the late 1970s and early 1980s with the Campaign Against Racism in the Media (see Hall, 1981) and programmes like *It Ain't Half Racist Mum* (BBC2, 1979) and the *Black and White Media Show* (see Twitchin, 1988). In the 1990s, recent initiatives include those undertaken by the Black Members Council of the National Union of Journalists, the International Media Working Group Against Racism and Xenophobia, the Commission for Racial Equality and members of the on-line ERAM network (Reading, 1999). The new Coalition for Asylum and Immigration Rights (CAIR) and the National Assembly Against Racism have been recently in active protest against press coverage of migrant issues. In addition, the criticism of racism in British news coverage of asylum-seekers by the European Commission against Racism and Intolerance (April 2001) was itself widely reported on news programmes on television, radio and in the press. The range of examples presented in this chapter, combined with evidence in Chapter 2 which showed one quarter of news items to be presenting negative racial messages of one form or another, does show the vital importance of persistent scrutiny of news output and the need to consistently question news producers' intentions and practices.

The decline in blatant explicit racism in news media, vividly illustrated by the dramatic decline in racist cartoons in the press and their increasing use to lampoon racism in wider society, does, however, indicate both the successes and limitations of this strategy. Success in achieving wider consensus on the evils of journalistic racism, and limitations as solely challenging racial bias in the news, may ignore key contextual issues. The significance of prevailing cultural, political and government discourse over race issues, the lack of minority ethnic staff in most news organisations, increasing recognition of anti-racism and multiculturalism in regulatory environments, problems with prevailing representations of both whiteness and blackness and competitive rivalry in news production all indicate the importance of developing more sophisticated and complex strategies for intervention and change. The development and character of anti-racist messages in the news is the subject of the next chapter.

4

Anti-Racism and the News

Introduction

The purpose of this chapter is to examine the meaning of anti-racism and the nature, extent and implications of anti-racism in news reporting. The primary focus here is British news, but a series of questions about the extent to which US news either denies or highlights racism, racial discrimination and ethnic diversity are also raised. In Chapter 2, about three-quarters of race-related news items were identified as broadly presenting an anti-racist message. Anti-racism has been defined rather narrowly and a-historically in the British context (Law, 1996), particularly through its linkage to municipal anti-racism in the 1980s. The term is used here, in a wider sense, to refer to media frames (Wolfsfeld, 1997) which seek to expose and criticise racist attitudes, statements, actions and policies, which address the concerns of immigrant and minority ethnic groups and show their contribution to British society, and which embrace an inclusive view of multicultural British identity. It has been established that media coverage of race issues in the British news has undergone a substantial shift in the last decade moving in many ways to become an 'anti-racist show'. The dominance of racist discourse, particularly in the press, in the 1980s has been replaced by a more ambivalent set of news messages, many of which contain and exhibit a preoccupation with exposing racism. This trend has run parallel to marked continuities in the transmission and reproduction of racist messages, which were demonstrated in Chapter 3.

This process of change may reflect a more untested set of propositions about a wider set of structural changes in ethnic relations in Britain. A wider shift in material conditions and political agendas which gave voice to issues of difference, diversity, cultural hybridity and multiple subjectivities through the 1980s and 1990s has been

111

examined elsewhere (Gilroy, 1990; Bonnett, 1993; Gillborn, 1995; Law, 1996; Modood, 1996; Mirza, 1997; Mac an Ghaill, 1999). Some of the key factors here include the increasing divergence of material conditions across ethnic minority groups, the exhaustion of municipal anti-racism, critiques of black homogeneity and renewed political, institutional and professional pressure for the recognition of ethnic difference from minority groups themselves. The resurgence of ethnicity as a totem in social and political movements combined with the rapidly shifting construction of new forms of hybrid cultural identity and theoretical reflection on the reworking and renewal of concepts of culture, ethnicity and ethnic identity have impacted unevenly across many arenas.

The rise of ethnic managerialism, which combines the privileging of ethnicity and ethnic diversity in British social policy and its intertwining with new managerialist ideas, in the 1990s has been identified (Law, 1996, 1997b; Mac an Ghaill, 1999). It has been seen to have established an important place in Benefits Agency policy, child-care policy, community-care policy and health policy amongst others. The attempt to construct 'consociationalism' (Lijphart, 1977) where the liberal democratic state accommodates ethnic pluralism, at the same time as attempts are being made to construct more ethnically exclusive criteria in the specification of citizenship in Britain and Europe, characterises not only the 'liberal settlement' of the 1960s but the appeal of the 'management of ethnic diversity' in the 1990s (Parekh, 1997). Increasing institutional and social engagement with ethnic and cultural diversity is acknowledged in a recent article by Stuart Hall, who proposes that this has led to a turning point in white people's perceptions of other ethnic groups in British society:

There are three key moments. The first was the Powell moment, when the notion of closure and a homogenous culture, of their culture versus ours, was at its height ... The second moment was when Tebbit issued the cricket test. People were very confused by it; they felt there was something in the argument, but they also sensed it didn't quite hold any longer. And now with Tebbit's latest outburst in October, they feel it's like a dinosaur speaking out, that it belongs to yesterday. [This refers to front-page coverage in the *Daily Mail* which referred to Norman Tebbit as a dinosaur due to his call for reassertion of white Englishness during the Conservative Party Conference in 1997 (MARCH OF THE DINOSAURS, 8 October 1997), also see Ferguson (1998) for a full discussion of Tebbit's statements.]

That doesn't mean Britain isn't still a racist society or people no longer attack black kids standing at bus stops. [This refers to the Stephen Lawrence case.] But it's as if Englishness has turned a corner . . . What we have, though, is a recognition that the terms have changed that the leading edge is moving to the side of cultural pluralism and diversity. (Hall and Jacques, 1997: 34)

The move to cultural pluralism and diversity that Hall tracks has happened at the same time as increasing critical questioning of the meaning of anti-racism. In the British context, anti–racism suffers from a range of problems. According to an overview by Mac an Ghaill (1999: 106), anti-racism is theoretically underdeveloped and has become overgeneralised and increasingly meaningless as the concept has been inflated to cover a wide range of phenomena; individual attitudes and actions, institutional policies and practices, political strategies, slogans and signs as well as popular forms of collective action. This parallels the criticism of the conceptual inflation of the notion of racism discussed in Chapter 1. The call then becomes one of focus, conceptual precision and disaggregation of situations, actions and outcomes. More simply, at its heart, anti-racism involves opposing racism. So, using the definition of racism established in Chapter 1, this means opposing any attempt to signify a collectivity as a 'race', opposing any attempt to attribute negative biological or cultural characteristics to a 'race', challenging the way racism 'makes sense' of the world for those who articulate it and challenging the 'unearned easy feeling of superiority' that racism provides. Such ideas may emerge in a range of historical, social and spatial contexts, and in debates over anti-racism there is likely to be a general tendency to understate its ubiquity and complexity. In examining anti-racist discourse and activities across international contexts a common theme has been evidence of tension between ideas of universalism and equal treatment, and ideas of diversity and different treatment.

More worryingly, Mac an Ghaill (1999) points to the ways in which anti-racism in practice has legitimised ethnic exclusion, and also to the increasing convergence of racist and anti-racist discourse across Europe. This position draws on the well-established critique that both anti-racism and racism both draw on mythical, culturally exclusive forms of human nature – for example white Englishness and the black victim (Gilroy, 1990; Solomos and Back, 1996; Law, 1996). Fieldwork with white youth is used by Mac an Ghaill to show these failings in the context of anti-racist policies and perceptions in schools, where such policy is seen as being 'informed by a principle of exclusivity' (1999:

142). This involves the lack of attention to the needs of ethnic groups other than Asians and African-Caribbeans, for example Irish and white English working-class students. The needs referred to here are 'cultural', identified for example in representation in curriculum material. The exclusion of concern for white students in the context of multicultural initiatives is seen as leading to a vacuum where white youth draw on and appropriate the language of anti-racism and represent themselves as the 'new victims' (whether this process refers to a more general experience of victimisation in compulsory state schooling or more specific racial victimisation as whites is unclear). Here class alienation and marginalisation is 'spoken through the language of racism'. Mac an Ghaill projects this argument further suggesting that we will see a 'discursive shift' in the media; with an increased focus on the racial problems of the social majorities as these 'new victims', and with a move away from attention to the racial problems of minorities.

The simplistic limitations of anti-racist discourse are well-established here, but this line of criticism raises a number of related questions. Firstly, how far is the reproduction of 'invisible' white culture in school teaching and learning environments underplayed in these accounts? It could easily be argued and demonstrated, as many studies of children's books have shown, that white culture is privileged, reinvented and dominant in curriculum materials, however absent it may be in explicitly multicultural initiatives. Secondly, how 'new' is this process? I recently overheard two little old ladies on a train in Bradford talking about that City Council's programmes of cultural events. One lady said; 'They never do anything unless its for the Asians, it'll become a no-go area for white people soon'. The views of these neat well-spoken ladies were unlikely to be 'new', and much more likely to have been often rehearsed and replayed in many conversations and over many years. The portrayal of poor white people as the victims of racial oppression by black and Asian migrants in Britain is of long- standing. The alleged letter from an elderly constituent who saw herself in this light was one of the key inspiration's for Enoch Powell's 'Rivers of Blood' speech. These sentiments can also be found in the anti-immigrant news items written by Nicholas Budgen in the 1997 General Election campaign where white Briton's are portrayed as 'strangers in their own land' (see Chapter 3). Similarly, trends amongst white youth of presenting themselves as victims of racial harassment in social spaces where minorities have fought to establish their day-to-day lives has been identified in varying social contexts. This was found to be a commonly expressed perception amongst white youngsters on some youth training schemes in central Leeds during discussion sessions led by myself about issues of racism and anti-racism in the late 1980s. Colin Webster (1995), in his longitudinal studies of youth attitudes in Keighley, West Yorkshire, shows this transition occurring through registered complaints of racial harassment. Here, the bulk of reported incidents initially came from Asian youths as they battled to establish residential and social networks in the town. This pattern was over-turned as increasing numbers of white youths presented themselves as victims of racial violence as ethnic spatial divisions became fixed, embedded and defended. Explaining racism as a 'perverted crusade' to protect white residential space appears as one key thread in news media explanations of the murder of Stephen Lawrence (see below).

Lastly, in the news media itself, how far has there been a move away from reporting the 'racial problems' faced by minority ethnic groups, with increased attention being given to reporting the racial problems of 'white victims'? It may be that selection of these groups of events for attention by news organisations reflects a common underlying theme; that of exposing racism particularly where it has a higher cultural proximity and unexpectedness (Fowler, 1991: 13). In consideration of the news items identified as 'exposing racism' in Chapter 2 it is clear that some newspapers such as the *Sun* and the *Daily Mail* did, on relatively infrequent occasions, play up the stories of white race victims – for example WHITE LAD DRIVEN OUT OF HOME BY RACISTS (*Sun*, 15 January 1997), RACE COUNCIL BIASED AGAINST WHITE MAN (*Daily Mail*, 17 December 1996). White people did appear in the news as victims of racial discrimination at work and victims of racial violence. Racist attitudes amongst black and Asian groups were also exposed, although this was more often shown as attitudes which were intolerant of other minority groups rather than those which were hostile to whites – for example SURVEY REVEALS RACIST STREAK IN ASIANS (*Guardian*, 5 February 1997). Such news messages were overwhelmingly drowned out by the regularity and frequency of items highlighting the problems of racism experienced by minority ethnic groups. So, no discernible shift to privilege the voices of white victims has been identified yet. Indeed, Mac an Ghaill's criticism of anti-racist discourse in school situations may be usefully applied to anti-racism in the news where organisations and journalists seem to be working within previously established discursive conventions of what anti-racism should be about, as opposed to elevating the 'unexpected'. The almost complete silence about the 'stupidity' and 'lunacy' of municipal anti-racism in the late 1990s, which had been a dominant news frame in the 1980s, is another indicator of the extent to which anti-racist discourse has permeated news organisations and may now be a more 'normal' news value itself. The Stephen Lawrence story dominated the news items examined during this study and the subsequent criticism of institutional racism and the renewal of confidence in anti-racist strategies may further strengthen this process. More detailed analysis of the news coverage which related to the Stephen Lawrence case during the period under study, November 1996 to May 1997, is presented below. This covered the key period of the inquest verdict and the call for a public inquiry prior to the General Election in May.

The Stephen Lawrence case

Case summary (1993–97)

Stephen Lawrence was a black, 18-year-old A-level student who was stabbed twice with a weapon, similar to a kitchen knife, through the chest and arm as he waited for a bus in Eltham, south-east London on 22 April 1993 by a group of white youths. He ran 130 yards with a punctured lung and paralysed arm before bleeding to death. During May/June 1993, five white youths were arrested and in July the Crown Prosecution Service dropped the charges against them. In April 1996 a private prosecution by the Lawrence family against three of the youths collapsed at the Old Bailey. In February 1997 the coroner's inquest was reopened and on 13 February gave a verdict of unlawful killing 'in an unprovoked racist attack by five white youths'. On 14 February the *Daily Mail* printed photos of the five youths on the front page under the headline 'Murderers', accusing them of killing Stephen Lawrence and suggesting that if this was libel then they should sue. This was found not to constitute statutory contempt by the Attorney General and the youths did not sue.

Media coverage

The bulk of media coverage of this case covered by this study was in February and March 1997. Media coverage was substantial and was accelerated by the action taken by the *Daily Mail* and its in-depth support for the Justice for Stephen Lawrence campaign. Seventy-seven items were identified with broadly equal proportions of items across tabloids, broadsheets, radio and television news. Only the broadsheets showed a roughly even level of coverage across different sources. Amongst the tabloids the *Daily Mail* chose to give a particularly high profile to this case with little attention by other such papers, and Radio 4 and Channel 4 gave greater coverage on radio and television respectively.

Media attacks on the white youths' right to silence

The *Independent*, *The Times*, the *Daily Mail*, the *Guardian* and the *Daily Telegraph* (12 February 1997) focused on the way in which the five young white men turned the inquest into a 'mockery of the legal system' by their claim, through the common law right of privilege of refusing to answer questions that might incriminate themselves, to remain silent and refuse to answer any questions including who they were; WALL OF SILENCE FROM WHITE YOUTHS AT LAWRENCE IN-QUEST, *Independent*.

News advocacy of racial justice and anti-racism

A BBC 2 Newsnight report (13 February 1997) was generally critical of the failure of the police and the criminal justice system to secure prosecution of those responsible for the murder. It included an interview with an Asian man who witnessed the attack whose comments were not reported elsewhere in the media, and interviews with some of Stephen's friends. In a studio discussion which followed, the Lawrence family's solicitor, a law lecturer and a barrister all agreed with the critique of the criminal justice system, and in addition wider references were made to the cases of a number of black people who died in police custody which was seen as affecting police relations with black communities.

BBC 1 News (13 February 1997) reported the inquest verdict and gave the bulk of item time to supporters of the Lawrence family. Both the family's solicitor and the coroner acknowledged that 'society' must confront and overcome racism. Channel 4 News (13 February 1997), in reporting the inquest verdict, gave particular prominence to Herman Ouseley, Chief Executive of the Commission for Racial Equality, stating that 'even the normally cautious CRE are demanding a public enquiry'. In reply, Herman Ouseley emphasised the negative impact on race relations and drew a parallel with the police response when Philip Lawrence (a white headteacher) was stabbed and murdered stating that this 'sends out the wrong message'. An item in the *People*, 16 February 1997, also took up this theme and claimed that the Stephen Lawrence case 'warranted only a quarter of mentions in national newspapers over 45 months that Philip Lawrence received in just 14 months'. The piece ends with the exhortation 'We must all strive to rid our society of the evil spectre of racism which threatens to destroy it'. Coverage of the verdict by Sky News was much more brief, but also critical of the justice system.

The Radio 4 Today programme 'What the Papers Say' repeated the view of the *Daily Mail* and the *Guardian* that the jury verdict was 'bad for race relations' (14 February 1997). A further report stated that one of the solicitors acting for one of the youths, whose photo appeared in the *Mail*, would not be suing the paper, and reaffirmed that Stephen Lawrence's murder was racially-motivated (15 February 1997). Subsequently an item discussed the implications of the *Daily Mail*'s action for 'racial harmony' and reported the perception that many black people 'felt they are not being treated fairly by the police or the media' (16 February 1997).

The *Guardian* front page on the inquiry verdict, which quoted the Coroner's words for its headline, UNLAWFULLY KILLED IN AN UN-PROVOKED RACIST ATTACK BY FIVE WHITE YOUTHS (14 February 1997), accompanied by a further item FAMILY'S FRUITLESS FIGHT FOR JUSTICE, was more careful and cautious in comparison to the *Daily Mail* although it thoroughly examined the injustice of the case.

A more 'balanced' view was given by Radio 1 news in that it quoted the Coroner who called Stephen Lawrence's murder a 'cold-blooded attack with racist motivations' and simultaneously defended the rights of the five white men whose photographs were used on the front page of the *Daily Mail* (14 February 1997).

Giving voice to a black mother

The announcement that the Lawrence family were to take further legal action, including complaints against the police and civil action against the five white youths, was also given prominence in the *Daily Telegraph*, *The Times* and the *Independent* (14 February 1997). The *Mirror* also covered this item and gave precedence to a statement from Stephen's mum which contained the accusation that the police let him bleed to death through taking no immediate medical action after being called to the scene; 'was it because they did not want to get their hands dirty with a black man's blood?' Stephen's mum's views were given prominence in a number of media items including an exclusive in the *Daily Mail* (7 February 1997) and a series of items on 11 February; such as MURDER MUM SLAMS 'RACIST' LEGAL SYSTEM, *Mirror*; WHITE JUSTICE FAILED MY SON and CRY FOR JUSTICE, *Daily Mail*; BRITAIN ALLOWS RACE MURDERS SAYS MOTHER, *Daily Telegraph*. Similar items appeared in *The Times* and the *Independent*. In the last of these items she is reported as saying that on her first visit to a police station she gave an officer a list of possible suspects who were involved. 'He folded the paper and rolled it into a ball. I asked him if he was going to put it in the bin. They were not taking my son's death as seriously as they should have done,' she said. In the *Guardian* item MOTHER ATTACKS 'RACIST' JUSTICE she is quoted as saying, 'My son was stereotyped by the police, he was black then he must be a criminal and they set about investigating him and us'. At the London launch of the European Year Against Racism, Doreen Lawrence spoke of 'Apartheid in London', *Guardian*, 19 February 1997.

The Daily Mail

In the same *Guardian* article, the chair of the anti-racist event Trevor Phillips praised the *Mail* saying that it had shown, 'that middle England might choose decency over bigotry'. In contrast the *Independent* refers to the '*Daily Mail* metamorphosing...into a sudden champion of downtrodden minorities', which it saw as 'rare and strange, refreshing and nauseating' (16 February 1997).

The *Daily Mail* decision to accuse the five youths of murder was discussed through letters from listeners on the Radio 4 PM programme (17 February 1997). All four letters quoted were in various ways critical of the paper. One listener accused the *Mail* of promoting racist attitudes, another criticised trial-by-tabloid, another denied the significance of racism emphasising instead youth envy, and the last listener more sympathetically compares the unfairness of the *Mail* with the unfairness of the attack itself and focuses criticism on the operation of criminal justice.

Support for pursuit of Stephen's killers by the *Mail* was given by Prime Minister John Major (Sky News, 18 February 1997) who said in

120 Race in the News

the Commons that there was 'no question of statutory contempt' as a result of the *Daily Mail* story.

Context and explanation

The *Daily Mail* gave a chronology of events under the headline, FAMILY'S FIGHT FOR JUSTICE (14 February 1997). This highlighted that Stephen Lawrence was the fourth black male to be murdered in the area in two years and that the gang shouted 'What, what nigger?' as they surrounded him. The Editorial Comment refers to 'A tragic failure of British justice', emphasising the seriousness of the newspaper's own condemnation of five men as murderers who have never been convicted in court and highlights racism as the sole motive for the murder. A further two-page spread in the same issue gave background on the local area with banner headlines:

WHY NEIGHBOURS WILL NOT SPEAK OUT AGAINST RACIST GANG
THE DAILY MAIL ACCUSES OF MURDERING STEPHEN LAWRENCE.
THE ESTATE STRUCK DUMB BY FEAR.
THERE ARE FEW BLACKS HERE. THOSE WHO MOVE IN MOVE OUT
SOON AFTER.

This story focuses on the criminal connections and gang mentality of the white youths in question and their effect on local people. A local resident is quoted as saying 'People here are disgusted with the attack on Stephen Lawrence, but they don't want to say anything publicly against the Acourts and their gang'. Also a representative of a local anti-racist group, the Greenwich Action Committee Against Racial Attacks, provided comment on the prevalence of racist violence and extreme Right activity in the local area.

This article also provides evidence from a secret police camera which was planted in the home of one of the youths which showed the youths practising knife attacks, making racist comments such as 'I reckon every nigger should be chopped up and left with nothing but fucking stumps', and laughing when the murder of Stephen Lawrence was discussed. This video footage was shown on a number of television news items including ITN News at Ten and BBC 1 9 O'clock News, 15 February 1997, which also acknowledged the problem of 'trial-by-media'.

A Radio 4 PM programme background report on the case highlighted the strength of BNP support in the local area and noted that the proportion of ethnic minority households in the area had dropped from 14 per cent to 2 per cent stating that 'race relations are tense' (16 February 1997), and a similar piece appeared in *The Times* (15 February 1997) with a highlighted quote from a local youth worker, 'We've been compliant too long, silence breeds racism'. The *Independent* sought explanations and referred to 'those who took furtive territoriality and turned it into a perverted crusade' (15 February 1997). The move of white households out of the East End to suburbs such as Eltham is seen as particularly due to the settlement of ethnic minority households in the inner city. The subsequent purchase of houses by such households in the suburbs is then resisted resulting in racist violence which in the case of Eltham has been successful in protecting 'white' residential space.

Conclusion

There is clear evidence here that there is no attempt on the part of the news media to undermine, deny or ignore the role and significance of racism in this case. Attention to and criticism of the racist motivation of the white youths in question despite their being legally innocent and not proven guilty is a strong and pervasive theme. There are also attempts, however uneven and inadequate, on the part of most sections of the media to contextualise and link this individual racism with wider material conditions and inequalities. This is a much weaker part of news coverage where there is ample room for improvement. The attention, space and sympathy given to Doreen Lawrence in news coverage is not only a testament to her strength and courage in speaking to the media, but also to way in which the views of a black British person have been unquestioningly accepted and reported. This is indicative of a wider acceptance of black people in a variety of roles across news coverage. The support for the Stephen Lawrence Campaign by the *Daily Mail* illustrates a clear commitment to using press power in the pursuit of racial justice, however suspect the motivation. It is indicative of the changing representation of race, particularly in comparison to the 1980s when racial attacks received little attention (van Dijk, 1991: 88). But, such anti-racist reporting is situated within the dominant discursive terrain of crime. This racialised context of crime news contains frequent linkages between race references, violence and dangerousness which therefore reflects the constrained and ambivalent meanings available to be drawn from this case.

The 'biggest sea change in media coverage of race', is how Michael Mansfield, the Stephen Lawrence family's QC, described the period during which the Public Inquiry was conducted (March 1998–February 1999), writing in the *Media Guardian* (19 April 1999). He notes the indifference of news organisations and current affairs programmes to the case early on (1993/94) compared to the extensive news, documentary and drama coverage more recently. Also, in relation to race crime more generally he recognises significant improvements in both local and national coverage. However, two particular trends are subject to criticism. Firstly, the way in which Granada Television and Talk Radio provided opportunities for the white youths to 'bare all' when they had arrogantly refused to do so at the Inquest, hence capitalising on the perpetrators of racism. Secondly, the simplification and reduction of the story through 'woolly thinking' to the twin themes of 'gross police incompetence' and 'institutional racism' rather than opening up a complex set of questions about human rights, freedom of information and education. More importantly in this context, he states that the 'media have found it impossible to ignore' Neville and Doreen Lawrence's pursuit of the 'highest human ideals – the right to life and the right to identity and respect'.

In an examination of one of the television documentaries that was shown, The Stephen Lawrence Story (Channel 4, February 1997), Jenny Owen confirms that there remains space for 'partial' not 'balanced', impassioned and 'political' documentary television, despite a context of increased competition signalled by the rise of the documentary soap (1999: 203). As Owen shows, this documentary drew on the stories of the police, the judiciary, the community, of young people and the Lawrences to present an interrogation of the meaning of multicultural citizenship in Britain. This documentary offered an engagement with the wider complex of questions about human rights which were found to be lacking in parts of news coverage. This model example of anti-racist television was recognised by an award from the Commission for Racial Equality in 1997.

The resurgence in anti-racist optimism that marked the publication of the Lawrence Inquiry report went hand-in-hand, however, with a resurgence in hostility, or backlash, which found expression in the letters columns and other articles in the press. 'The Lawrence inquiry report is a biased, politicised smear of the police' wrote Cllr William MacDougall (Conservative, Haringey) (*Guardian*, 2 March 1999). Alan Clark, MP (Conservative), referred to the inquiry as producing an 'inquisition of McCarthyite proportions' (*Daily Telegraph*, 4 March 1999), and the *Daily Mail* carried articles about the irrelevance of judicial race training. Lord Dholakia criticised this process and warned of wider problems to come, during presentations to the Labour Party and Liberal Democrat Party Conference Fringe Meetings on 'Lawrence What Next?':

> Following the Stephen Lawrence Inquiry, there has been a rapid process of change. The challenge to us all is to sustain the process in the face of a media backlash, diminishing public interest, institutional inertia and the traditional working practices of criminal justice organisations. (Reported in NACRO Race Unit Newsletter, no. 19, Summer 1999)

Exposing institutional racism

One of the key messages to arise from the Stephen Lawrence Inquiry was that:

> Racism, institutional or otherwise, is not the prerogative of the Police Service. It is clear that other agencies including those dealing with housing and education also suffer from the disease. If racism is to be eradicated there must be specific and co-ordinated action both within the agencies themselves and by society at large, particularly through the educational system, from pre-primary school upwards and onwards. (Home Office, 1999: para 6.54)

The extent to which the news media actively assist in revealing and exposing institutional racism across all spheres of society is both a reflection of anti-racist activity in wider society, and a benchmark of anti-racist values within news organisations. The pattern of news reporting covering these types of items, in the period subject to intensive study (November 1996–May 1997), reflects a number of factors: tremendous unevenness in organisational efforts to tackle institutional racism across differing sectors of society; the effectiveness of the CRE in carrying out formal investigations of key institutions; the efforts of individuals in pursuing complaints of racial discrimination; and editorial and journalistic decisions about what to report. Partly as a result of this combination of factors, the largest group of items of this type concerned the Stephen Lawrence case. The second largest group of news items exposing racism of various sorts was in the sport context and this primarily covered racist comments made by managers and players in football (see Chapter 2). This partly reflects the campaigning efforts of those involved in various initiatives to challenge racism in football and their success in involving leading black players in news events., However, many of these items did not reflect news media exposure of a depth of ingrained racism in sports institutions, unlike that of the Armed Forces discussed below. The third-largest category related to the question of racism is the NHS. This issue, which had great potential significance, was however raised rather obliquely, being thrown into the news spotlight by the reporting of Diane Abbott's (Labour MP) comments criticising the employment of white, blue-eyed Finnish nurses in a London hospital (Hackney) sited in an area which contains significant black and Asian communities. This gave a tremendous opportunity to the tabloids to 'expose' the racism of a black Labour MP, which they did with great relish. However problematic, these comments did generate significant news debate on issues of racism in the NHS which would otherwise probably have been ignored. Many public-sector institutions have remained impervious to and insulated from anti-racist intervention, particularly due to their lack of democratic accountability and the failure of successive governments to pursue an effective racial-equality agenda. In these respects the NHS and the Armed Forces are remarkably similar, only beginning to be exposed to criticism and intervention over these matters in the 1990s. News coverage of racism in the Armed Forces is a particularly interesting example as here there was sustained exposure of cases of racism experienced by black and Asian soldiers as well as significant coverage of institutional racism.

Military racism

Case summary

The Commission for Racial Equality has been pursuing a racial equality action programme with the Ministry of Defence following a number of cases of racial discrimination within the Armed Forces, including that of Sergeant Jacob Malcolm who was barred from transfer to the Life Guards section of the Household Cavalry in 1991 because he was black. The threat of legal action being taken by the CRE against the MoD, in the form of a non-discrimination notice, combined with details of particular cases and findings from an independent enquiry in March 1997 provided a range of news material.

News coverage

The news media reported these issues and 30 items appeared from January to March 1997. Half of these were found in the broadsheets, a quarter in the tabloids and the remaining items were covered on radio and television. All reported criticism of racism in the Armed Forces, and comment, for example in editorials in *The Times* and the *Guardian*, amplified this criticism. Little room, if any, was given to counter claims or defensive comment by the MoD or senior ranking officers.

The Times carried the most items (7) dealing with this case. In January four items were found in the same edition of *The Times*, 30 January 1997. The key theme of this reporting was that measures to improve recruitment of blacks and Asians into the Armed Forces had failed and that service chiefs were to take new initiatives; SERVICES' ANTI-RACISM PLAN FAILS TO BOOST RECRUITMENT. *The Times* leader emphasised that 'racialism is as repugnant in the Armed Forces as in any other aspect of public or private life' and further that 'bigotry must be met with the same steel in the military as in any other profession'. The sensitivity of the CRE is acknowledged in its efforts to shift indifference to issues of racism in the Armed Forces. Later in March a more in-depth piece gave substantial coverage to an MoD commissioned report carried out by a private consultancy which found a 'huge complacency' over racism (OFFICERS UNDER FIRE FOR TOLERATING RACISM IN SERVICES, 21 March 1997). This was seen to be underlain by 'anxiety that the comfortable lifestyle of the white majority could be threatened'. Attempts to recruit more ethnic-minority personnel, particularly into the Navy were 'denigrated as political correctness'. Black sailors were seen to be afraid of water, unwilling to fight and lacking in qualifications. In the Army black people were said to be 'lazy' and Asians were seen to be 'sly'. The RAF was found to have an 'unwritten rule of no blacks, Pakis, spots or specs on VIP parades'. The only reported comment of an MoD official was to acknowledge the serious issues involved. The role of the CRE was again highlighted in March (26 March 1997) under the headline RACE CHIEFS MAINTAIN LEGAL THREAT AGAINST ARMED FORCES, which reported that the CRE would suspend serving a non-discrimination notice as some training and recruitment initiatives were being taken. There was no quote from the MoD, and the CRE legal adviser commented on the lack of a 'sense of urgency' and the 'pervasive, long-running and deeply entrenched problem of racism'.

A *Guardian* editorial commenting on the MoD consultants' report refers to the revolving door whereby black troops are recruited, physically and verbally abused and then leave (21 March 1997). It, unlike *The Times* editorial, expresses reservations with the CRE's equal-opportunities approach pointing a finger instead at the significance of the class system. *The Times* referred to a 'military ethos' where 'the Army must be allowed to educate its own'. Both drew parallels with the American experience where issues of tackling racial segregation and opening up opportunities for promotion for black people have been key features of debates about the Armed Forces.

The *Daily Mail* followed up its 'exclusive revelation' about widespread racism in the services with a half-page piece on the case of Iftkhar Mirza whose complaint was still under investigation by the Army after 14 months at the time of writing, entitled PREJUDICE ON PARADE. This item relates his experiences, and the sub-heading states WHEN I COMPLAINED SQUADDIES IN KLU KLUX KLAN ROBES BEAT ME UP (17 March 1997). This incident is expanded upon in the text which states that he was injured so badly he had to be taken into protective custody. His story is illustrated with long quotes recounting his 'claims' and two head-and-shoulders pictures. One of these was from early on in his career in uniform, when he was a 'top student earmarked for promotion', and the other shows him now looking disconsolate with the caption 'hounded from the Army'. He recounts 14 years of racial harassment and racial discrimination which drove him out of the Army, and the comments of a new sergeant at training camp who said 'I'm not going to have a Paki on my first passing-out parade'. On his transfer to the Royal Army Medical Corps in Aldershot his wife stated that she was generally referred to as 'WOP – wife of Paki'.

TV features

The showing of two features on racism in the Services, firstly on the Black Britain programme (26 March 1997), and secondly on Channel 4's Dispatches programme (20 March 1997), gave additional impetus to news reporting. The *Daily Telegraph* referred to the former programme in its coverage noting that it indicated widespread distrust about complaints of racial discrimination and racial harassment which were experienced by over 50 per cent and 33 per cent of black soldiers respectively. Of these, only 13 per cent were found to have made a formal complaint. The *Independent* gave greater space to material shown in the Dispatches programme, 'Racism in the Army'. Cases examined in the programme were reported including that of Solomon Raza which is described as the 'most bizarre' because he was abused and beaten on a daily basis during training because his father was Pakistani.

Overall, this coverage reinforces the claim that news media tend to see 'exposing racism', particularly in institutional contexts where little has been previously reported, as particularly newsworthy. In this case, the role of the CRE cannot be underestimated. Challenging institutional racism in the Armed Forces is one of the key successes that the organisation has achieved under Sir Herman Ouseley's leadership. Skilful use of news media by the CRE to promote this objective is also evident. What is particularly remarkable in the news items is the little weight given to arguments opposing this objective, for example denials of racism, criticism of the CRE or criticism of individual black soldiers.

Fashion industry racism

There have been long-standing criticisms of the racist exclusion of black women from a wide variety of roles in theatre, ballet, television, advertising and fashion (Bourne, 1995; Young, 1996). Racism in the fashion industry has prospered through a conspiracy of silence amongst agents, models and photographers with little emerging onto news agendas. A high-profile voice that challenged this institutional silence was that of Naomi Campbell whose critical comments were reported in depth in April 1997, PREJUDICED FASHION BOSSES INSULT ME AS THE BLACK BARDOT (*Sun*, 11 April 1997). This story was covered in both the tabloids and the broadsheets and provided easy and appealing linkages to be made between celebrity, race and the female body. An 'anti-racist show' of sympathetic coverage of these comments from the press was not enough to constitute a serious challenge to the industry. These comments could be easily dismissed as 'the un-substantiated carping of the tantrum-prone rich and famous' (Gary Younge, THE TRENDS THAT MAKE BEAUTY SKIN DEEP, *Guardian*, 24 November 1999).

The BBC programme Macintyre Undercover provided incontrovert-
ible evidence that racism in the fashion industry was endemic, and
further evidence from footage not used in the programme was reported
in the *Guardian* (RACE BIAS ATTACK ON TOP MODEL AGENCY, 24
November 1999). Hostile references to black models as 'niggers', dis-
like of black women in general and systematic exclusion from modelling opportunities, for example in Milan, were shown as prevalent
features of the world's largest modelling agency, Elite, and in particular the views of its top executives. This provides some explanation for
the lack of response to Naomi Campbell's earlier criticisms as this is
the agency that represents her. The rationale that racism must 'make
sense of the world for those who use it', as argued in Chapter 1, is also
borne out here. The exclusion of black models from the covers of
fashion magazines, and in particular the removal of Naomi Campbell
from the cover of American Vogue which prompted her comments, is
seen as common business sense as the 'sales drop by 20 per cent', as a
spokesman for Jean-Paul Gaultier once said (Gary Younge, *Guardian*,
24 November 1999).

This case highlights the value and significance of committed investi-
gative documentary-making and the vital role that responsible anti-
racist journalism can play. The Macintyre Undercover series had
previously exposed the integral links between extreme-right groups
like Combat 18 and violent groups associated with football such as
Chelsea's Headhunters. In the programme on the fashion industry,
exposing racism was a secondary theme with much greater attention
to the pervasive sexual exploitation of young girls in modelling. The
use of such covert video recording has proved a powerful tool; being
invaluable in revealing police brutality and racism in the case of
Rodney King in Los Angeles and in revealing the ways in which
vicious racism was played out in the home in the Stephen Lawrence
case. But, the extent to which Macintyre Undercover will prompt
significant change in the fashion industry's complacency about institutional racism remains to be seen. The hostility to criticism from
within the fashion industry was illustrated by the almost complete
silence of the fashion press. Vogue's online magazine, *Vogue Daily*,
did however report the suspension of three of Elite's senior executives
(*Guardian* Editor, 26 November 1999). Reporting of the story in the
Daily Mail and in the *Yorkshire Post* completely ignored the issue of
racism and played up the story of a white model who was shown as
being heavily involved in drug abuse. This fickle attention to issues of

racism here indicates the speed with which conventional concerns with anti-racism can be either harnessed to the market concerns of news organisations or swept aside by other interests. A more certain trend is the generally increasing role that minority individuals and organisations play in making race news in Britain, and this is examined below.

Exposing racism in US news

In the recent US study of race and media (Entman and Rojecki, 2000) we find little hard evidence of the attention given by news media to exposing racism, whereas there is much useful reflection on the ways in which coverage can or should be improved. Is there a lack of such items because news media are complicit in the process of denying racism and racial discrimination? Or is this because this aspect of news coverage is seen as not central to Entman and Rojecki's chosen thematic analysis, hence it has not been adequately researched so far? Or is this because there is actually little US news coverage which exposes racism and highlights the benefits of ethnic diversity for other reasons?

In their analysis of the coverage of poverty they do note the important equation of poverty with suffering, by repeated reference in news items to racial discrimination, racism and police brutality (2000: 252). However, it is suggested that the connection between these two issues, poverty and racism, was rarely explained and also that it was frequently suggested that discrimination was common in previous decades and was 'over and done with long ago'. This material evaluating poverty and its linkages with other threats – crime, violence and drugs – or suffering – racism, unemployment and homelessness – draws on news coverage from 1990 and 1993/4. As such, US news is depicted as abetting denial of racism and discrimination. But, is this the whole story? Are most news depictions of instances of racism in American society framed so as to deny their contemporary significance and importance? This question is examined here through the use of a limited and selective set of recent examples.

On 5 September 2000, the *Chicago Tribune* and WGN television news reported on the case of a long-running racial discrimination suit against R.R. Donnelly and Sons, a printing plant in Dwight, Illinois. This case was front-page news in the Business Section, BIAS COMPLAINT PUT IN NEW LIGHT. The central picture is of one of the key

figures in the class-action lawsuit, Alan Roundtree, who is shown in
church (he is an interim minister) smiling and holding the hand of an
elderly seated African-American woman as if being congratulated for
his role in this story. The headline reads:

> Testimony from current and future R. R. Donnelly employees is bringing to
> life charges of racism contained in a discrimination suit against the printing
> giant. Allegations include white workers dressing as Klansmen and wearing
> blackface. (*Chicago Tribune*, 5 September 2000)

Rita Harrison, another black worker, told of a flier that circulated in
her Donnelly place of work in Indiana spelling out the rules of an
imaginary 'hunting season' targeting black people. Racist graffiti,
racial discrimination in hiring, promotion and redundancy (for
example when 31 per cent of white workers and only 1 per cent of
575 black workers were relocated) and regular racist abuse are presented forcefully and sympathetically in this article. Rather than the
journalists' news coverage being in denial of racism, it gives voice to
the lead attorney for the black workers who said about the company:

> They're in denial. [Donnelly] has a culture that is racist and its workers have
> endured treatment that is really outrageous.

The article arose through coverage of new testimony being filed which
documents the black workers' experiences. The piece does acknowledge
the vagaries of news coverage noting that the case initially drew headlines three years ago when it was filed and had subsequently been
forgotten by the media. Overall, the coverage of this case indicates a
variety of features. Firstly, there is concern to present a serious account
of a major case of employer discrimination. Secondly, the evidence,
voice and images of black workers are foregrounded, sub-lines highlighted that in the face of everyday 'racial put-downs' you 'just put your
armor on'. Thirdly, denials from company management are presented
as such with no supporting comment. This example does illustrate that
there are items which do not 'fit' the picture presented above. Clearly,
discrimination cases such as this can be read by some as black people
'whining' and blaming employers for their own faults, but that does not
imply that such news coverage abets denial of racism generally.

On 6 November 2000, *Newsweek* reported on violent racist attacks
against Korean- and Asian-Americans, THE NEW VICTIMS OF HATE,

BIAS CRIMES HIT AMERICA'S FASTEST GROWING ETHNIC GROUP. The picture used to illustrate this story shows a smartly dressed young Korean-American, John Lee, who suffered a fractured skull after being beaten outside his dormitory at State University of New York, Binghamton, and he was told 'you damned Chink, that's what you get'. The caption reads: Scared. 'I could have died out there, the system let me down'. This story uses John Lee's case to illustrate publication of a report from a coalition of Asian-American civil-rights groups about increasing reporting of violent attacks. The article criticises the stereotype of Asian-Americans as ultra-successful and the associated denial of racism, aimed at this, group by the FBI, the police and also other black and Latino students. The comments of the President of the Asian Student Union at SUNY are highlighted in the article:

> People think if you're Asian you're automatically interning for Merrill Lynch and you're never touched by racism. (Rizalene Zabala, student activist)

This article gives voice to Asian-Americans, criticises institutional racism and exposes little-reported violent racism; there is no evidence here of denial.

A further argument that Entman and Rojecki make is the failure of US news coverage to report the persistence of racial advantage that accrues to whites, for example the invisibility of white preference in university entrance for the children of college benefactors and alumni. This may indeed be so and is particularly evident in the debates over affirmative action, which are discussed further in Chapter 5. In this context, it is interesting to note Ellis Cose's article in *Newsweek* (18 September 2000) which chooses to focus on the advantages of whiteness, WHAT'S WHITE ANYWAY. This is not to discount the argument but to suggest that such news items must also be fitted into our understanding of the 'big picture' of news coverage. This article focuses on the historical need to claim whiteness in order to access citizenship in the USA. It traces the decline and erosion of the 'specialness of whiteness'; here Cose may fall foul of Entman and Rojecki's claim that this contributes to a denial of durable white privilege. In addition, in rather general terms the item argues that race science has been thrust aside and that we are faced with the problem of how to reduce racial categories to the 'irrelevance they deserve'. Such speculation is at odds with the title of the *Newsweek* special in which this article appeared, REDEFINING RACE IN AMERICA (18 September 2000) discussed in more detail in Chapter 3; are we being asked to redefine or totally reject race-thinking? The thrust of the special edition is acknowledgement of the increasing number of people who have mixed ethnic and cultural backgrounds. Here a key social shift in the USA was argued to involve a move away from race towards ethnic diversity. This could be seen to encompass a lessening of both attention on, and the continued existence of, racism and racial discrimination. Linguistic cues refer to 'America the blended', the 'Age of Color' and a 'multiplicity of ethnic forces'. A reader's letter printed in the 9 October edition of *Newsweek* confirms Entman and Rojecki's point:

> Your special report on race was so eager to describe how race had changed that it neglected to tell how it hasn't. Black people in the US continue to fare worse than whites in accumulated wealth, life expectancy, unemployment, imprisonment rates and other significant social indicators. (Joel Olson, Phoenix, Arizona)

In fairness, a passing reference in the main item, THE NEW FACE OF RACE, does make this precise point, but it is swept aside in discussion of the 'tricky cross-currents' of colour. There is also attention here to renewal of anti-Hispanic racism arising in response to immigration from Mexico, which further contradicts assertions of journalistic denial.

News actors

Improving space for minority voices

Analysis of selected sources from the British press in the 1980s showed that in only 3.8 per cent of items on minority ethnic affairs were groups allowed to speak for themselves (van Dijk, 1993: 254). From November 1996 to May 1997 the various individuals and organisations which were reported as the central actors of each race-related news story, being either mentioned specifically or shown visually, were recorded. Ethnic minorities and related organisations were the primary news actors in 23 per cent of items. This category covers a variety of people and a breakdown is given in Table 4.1 below.

Table 4.1   Minority news actors

Actors	%	No.
Individual blacks and Asians	27.4	83
Sports figures and celebrities	23.8	72
Immigrants and asylum-seekers	21.8	66
Campaigners and CRE	14.2	43
Minority religious groups:	10.9	33
Muslims, Hindus, Jews		
MPs and parliamentary candidates	1.9	6
Total	100	303

The accusation of lack of ethnic minority 'voice' in the media in previous decades (see Chapter 2) does not appear to hold in the 1990s; minority people and organisations are making and defining the news in a significant proportion of items. Access does seem to have markedly improved although many issues about the form and content of coverage clearly still remain. Given that this analysis covered the General Election, the two major political parties were also key news actors. But, the Conservative Party was more likely to be making race news than the Labour Party as reflected in its comparative prominence in items (14.5 per cent to 6.6 per cent). This reflects particularly the stronger bid for the ethnic minority vote by the Conservatives through the news media, and the relatively 'quiet' approach of the Labour Party on race and immigration issues. All the other political parties made a very low showing in race items including the extreme right.

The prominence of criminal justice representatives – police, judges and so on – as central news actors in over 7 per cent of items reflects the focus of news attention on crime generally. Other key institutional news actors were the NHS (due to the Diane Abbott story) and other employers which reflects the widespread news coverage of racial discrimination at work.

Academics and researchers are a further key group of news actors who are shaping and defining race news. There was much coverage of research on racial attitudes with an emphasis on exposing the persistence of racism amongst young people, for example YOUNG BRITAIN: BIGOTED, RACIST, BOASTING ABOUT SEX (*London Evening Standard*, 5 February 1997), BRITAIN'S YOUTH THE MOST INTOLERANT IN EUROPE

(*Guardian*, 6 February 1997) and NATION OF SELF-INDULGENT XENO-
PHOBES (*Independent*, 21 November 1996).

Agendas for action

The disjuncture between the world of news and the world of social
action is particularly evident in the reporting of demands and claims
for intervention and action on issues of racism, racial discrimination,
racial and ethnic inequalities and cultural difference. There is a wealth of
activity, energy and innovation evident in the various forms of community-based minority ethnic organisations. These organisations have
engaged for many years in a diverse range of forms of intervention in
these issues, either separately or in collaboration with other public
services (Hylton, 1998), with concerns in education and training, housing and homelessness, welfare and poverty, physical and mental health,
personal social services, sports and leisure, music and arts and criminal
justice. These increasingly strong social networks frequently express
demands that intertwine the triple objectives of cultural difference,
equality and anti-racism. Yet little of their activities surfaces in the
news. This may reflect limited attempts on the part of minority organisations and individuals to use the news media and limited efforts on the
part of journalists to investigate what is being done in this arena. The
rapidly expanding variety of forms of minority-led news output, due
partly to concerns with and criticisms of the output of major news
services, parallels forms of minority ethnic organisation in many other
spheres of society where a failure of a mainstream sector to provide a
relevant and appropriate service prompts the expansion of minority-led
provision.

   Dominant claims for action by minorities which do appear in the
mainstream British news media have been about challenging institutional racism in a wide variety of contexts; calling for equal treatment
at work, justice before the law, improvements in the rights of migrants,
stronger race-relations legislation and actions to improve educational
opportunities (see Chapter 2). In the context of General Election news,
these minority-led agendas were frequently displaced by the non-spe-
cific wider concerns of the main political parties and their interests and
chances of capturing minority ethnic votes. Attempts by a coalition of
minority organisations to push an explicitly anti-racist set of concerns
onto news agendas was a dismal failure. Adverts were placed in the
press that summarised these concerns, for example RACE FOR THE

ELECTION (*Guardian*, 17 April 1997); this illustrates the fragmented character of minority ethnic news, the centrality of normative whiteness in news production and a political environment where relatively fragile national alliances established to promote anti-racism can easily be marginalised.

Conclusion

The 'great anti-racist show' is live and kicking in British news, and, as with many forms of entertainment, tried and tested formulas prevail. News organisations and journalists do seem to be working within previously established discursive conventions of what anti-racism should be about, as opposed to elevating the 'unexpected' and pushing forward the serious debate over how to fundamentally shift British racism. Anti-racist rhetoric is strong and exposing the stupidity of racism does make front-page news – for example TOTAL ECLIPSE OF THE LOON (*The Mirror*, 11 August 1999, in an article about Prince Phillip's comment about the technological ineptness of Indians). Here, there is a recurring tendency to refer to the racist comments of public figures as 'gaffes'; ingrained racism is thus reduced to an unconscious indiscreet blunder. Do these individuals (Prince Phillip, Geoffrey Archer, Jack Straw) really not know what they are saying? Further, it is such 'unwitting stereotyping' that has been taken to be the driving force for systematic institutional racism in the Lawrence Inquiry. Nevertheless, it is better to see racism ridiculed in the news, than anti-racism. There is an almost complete silence about the 'stupidity' and 'lunacy' of anti-racism policies and initiatives in the late 1990s. The dominant news frame in the 1980s has gone and this does indicate the extent to which anti-racist discourse has permeated news organisations and may now be a more 'normal' news value itself. As yet, the further shift in race news forwards (or backwards) to an increasing focus on the problems of white individuals and groups 'spoken through the language of racism' (Mac an Ghaill, 1999) has not taken place. However, we are unlikely to see this phase in news reporting continue in the same form given the volatile, ambivalent and fickle character of this 'anti-racist show'. The racially ambivalent character of US news is also evident. There is material to suggest that US news media are also engaging in an 'anti-racist show', highlighting violent racism, exposing cases of racial discrimination and talking-up the 'cool' nature of ethnic and cultural mixing.

The Stephen Lawrence story dominated the British news items examined during the case study period and was described as the 'biggest sea change in media coverage of race', by Michael Mansfield QC (*Media Guardian*, 19 April 1999). He notes the indifference of news organisations and current-affairs programmes to the case early on (1993/94) compared to the extensive news, documentary and drama coverage more recently. Also, in relation to race crime more generally he recognises significant improvements in both local and national coverage. What this sea change will bring in terms of trends in race news is uncertain and unknown. At best, we can expect courage, innovation and creativity in identifying institutional racism and forms of racial, ethnic and cultural exclusion. A recent case from Sweden illustrates the campaigning role that the media can take, in this case in seeking to expose the extreme right. Here, four national newspapers joined together to combat rising neo-Nazi violence by publishing photographs and names of 54 allegedly active members of neo-Nazi groups, and the same editorial condemned their actions. The allegation by the papers that all these individuals were responsible for acts of violence for which they had not been convicted broke an unwritten rule in the Swedish media which did provoke some criticism (*International Herald Tribune*, 4–5 December 1999).

In Britain the overall picture of institutional racism that emerged from news coverage highlighted the immigration service, criminal justice organisations, football clubs, health authorities and trusts, the armed forces and private employers like Fords as key problem areas. Some attention was given to racism in churches, schools, Fire Services, entertainment, fashion, airlines and other employers. There is no silence here about the range and diversity of institutional racism and racism is not simply reduced to the problem of racist individuals as some critics have suggested (Gordon and Rosenberg, 1989). The improved news coverage of anti-racist campaigning activity is a key change since the 1980s which reflects an increased openness to minority voices. British news and documentary-making contains a powerful thread of output that does excel in carrying these messages and debates forward, for example many of Gary Younge's pieces in the *Guardian* inspire and enthuse in this regard. The renewal of confidence in anti-racist voices together with strong anti-racist political leadership may further strengthen and deepen this process across the news media. At worst, we will see a simple retreat where it will become fashionable again to pour vitriol on attempts to challenge racism, and where backward-looking forms of cultural affirmation provide strong, entirely 'sensible' justifications for advocating both racial and cultural purity together with hatred and exclusion of those outside the white nation. These outcomes may also be significantly influenced by the extent to which news organisations have an ethnically-diverse workforce. Initiatives to promote such representation are considered in the next chapter.

5

Citizenship, Positive Action and the News Media

Citizenship tests

Citizenship discourse is characterised by a series of tensions and dichotomies (Lister, 1997). The liberal political tradition encourages a focus on the status of being a citizen with a set of civil, political, social and reproductive individual rights. The civic republican tradition emphasises that citizenship involves a set of active duties and obligations. More recently the attention to citizens' duties and obligations has been recast as drawing upon an 'ethic of care', which emphasises the responsibilities that stem from specific caring relationships particularly in the private sphere, and this is counterposed to an 'ethic of justice' which attends to rights in more public spheres (Gilligan, 1982; Tronto, 1993). Citizenship is also a key terrain within which boundaries of inclusion and exclusion have been constructed both within nation-states and between citizens and other outsiders, be they resident or not. A further dichotomy in the construction of citizenship is between universalism and difference. Citizenship rights are often presented as universal and therefore inherently resistant to claims for attention to and respect for difference and diversity. A key theme emerging from Lister's work is to seek a critical synthesis of these fundamental tensions of rights/duties, care/justice, inclusion/exclusion and universalism/difference within citizenship theory and citizenship praxis informed by the principle of inclusiveness.

In the evaluation of positive action initiatives, projects and programmes, these theoretical and conceptual frameworks of citizenship can be operationalised to produce a core set of tests or questions. To what extent have these programmes:

- led to the development, establishment or extension of various individual or group rights?
- led to increased active participation in duties, obligations and care?
- led to decreases in social, political and economic exclusion and increases in social, political and economic inclusion?
- led to improvements in the recognition of and respect for ethnic difference within a framework of universal rights?

Tested against these yardsticks, the British experience of positive action shows that in a number of ways citizenship has been enhanced. Advocating the expansion of positive-action initiatives based on arguments about the renewal of citizenship, as opposed to compensation-based arguments, may provide new ways to challenge political and social opposition to positive action in Europe and affirmative action in the USA. This chapter examines the meaning of positive action in the UK context, its impact on news media and issues for operation and practice.

Positive action

Background

Positive action has been lawful in Britain for 22 years and there has been little thorough evaluation of its social, economic and political impact despite the development of an enormous variety of often small initiatives, projects and programmes (Law and Harrison, 1999). Thousands of individuals from black and minority ethnic communities have progressed through positive-action programmes, yet in a recent study of the British experience Edwards (1995) concludes that lack of data has severely hindered assessment of output effects. Appraisal has been all the more difficult since positive action could blur into other kinds of anti-racist work, and may have focused on individuals, local area-based populations, religious or community bodies, potential service-providers, or specified categories of person. Interpretations of positive action embrace a variety of enterprises aimed at changing the involvement of minorities individually or collectively. The phrase has implied direct intervention by or through administrative and financial mechanisms to alter existing patterns. The concept could be disaggregated in terms of its goals, which might include helping to increase real equality in individuals' opportunities, bringing previously excluded groups up to a universal level, assisting cultural diversity, and others. The present political climate provides significant opportunities for enhancement, expansion and innovation in these programmes, particularly through their development into sectors that have so far been untouched.

The election of a New Labour Government in 1997 raised the prospect of a more sympathetic approach to positive-action strategies across a range of policy domains. There were expectations of change, despite a degree of silence on race during the General Election. This silence was broken by Tony Blair's reference to the need to allow 'all the talents of the people to shine through' at the Labour Party Conference in October 1997. The *Guardian* provided an analysis of ETHNIC EQUALITY, A BEACON BURNING DARKLY (2 October 1997) and reported the key role played by the CRE in lobbying for explicit attention to racial and ethnic equality issues, particularly in the Civil Service. The issue of black minority ethnic participation within police forces and other areas of public employment has subsequently had a very high profile, stimulated especially by debate about the Lawrence case (see *Sociological Research Online*, 4(1), March 1999). At the same time New Labour has confirmed an existing trend for the acknowledgement of cultural sensitivity and competence as important concerns in addressing needs and providing services. This connects with an increasing official recognition of ethnic differences beyond the black/white divide, as well as reflecting an understanding that shared experiences of racism may generate particular needs for black minorities by contrast with white households.

Yet positive-action strategies aimed at bringing more minority ethnic people through into jobs, policy arenas, education and training are by no means new. They have been on the agenda for many years and have taken a variety of forms. During the Conservative period of office (1979–97) there were highly significant developments in institutional practices aimed at opening up organisations and networks to more black minority ethnic participants. Thus, while support for affirmative action may have become less certain in the USA after an initial strong impetus, Britain has gradually been accumulating a set of experiences which could be built on. (USA affirmative action programme outcomes have recently been examined by Bowen and Bok (1998), and Gabriel (1998) has reviewed political campaigning over affirmative action.) The UK is in direct contrast to France and Germany where such strategies have yet to secure significant political or governmental support (Joppke, 1999; Calves and Sabbagh, 1999). Direct and sustained political opposition to specific programmes has been relatively muted in the UK. On the other hand, central government rarely prioritised programmes forcefully from 1979 to 1997, and there was little substantial in-depth monitoring or detailed research on outcomes. In Britain, therefore, it is of particular importance to evaluate the impact of positive-action initiatives. In other words to assess what works for whom and in what context and, moreover, to identify and demonstrate the wider contribution these programmes have made to improvements in the overall quality of life across different communities as well as highlighting negative features and consequences. Positive-action strategies can be usefully linked to questions about universality, fragmentation and particularism, thus highlighting concerns for daily practice.

One way of looking at positive-action strategies is as means of adjusting or countering societal differentiation, and thereby making mainstream citizenship expectations more accessible to others. Thus programmes can be interpreted as changes through which apparently universalistic practices are renegotiated and made more responsive to difference, through which negative discrimination is countered, or through which practices in employment or service provision are altered in ways that put people on a more equal footing. At the same time, however, positive-action strategies can raise difficult questions about universality of treatment. On the one hand they may seek to make citizenship experiences more even across differing groups of people in general, but on the other may draw distinctions between people from different backgrounds. When particularistic claims – related for instance to ethnicity – are inserted into the debate, the challenge to universality becomes more complex, raising concerns about new privileges while seeking to accommodate cultural sensitivities. Particularism – which in this context refers to claims for distinctive rights or treatment for specific groups or categories of people – raises serious questions about fairness and inclusion (see Spicker, 1993/94).

Comparison with a recently tightened definition of affirmative action in the USA helps to put the UK experience in context. In the USA, clarification of the meaning of affirmative action was provided to heads of executive departments and agencies by the White House in 1995 following a Presidential Affirmative Action Review (www.whitehouse.gov/WH/EOP/OP/html/aa/ap-a.html). Here, race, ethnicity or gender preferences in the provision of mainstream jobs, services and contracts is lawful provided that programmes do not create quotas, do not create preferences for unqualified individuals, do not create reverse discrimination or continue after equal opportunity purposes have been achieved. The recent *Adarand Constructors, Inc.* v. *Pena* case has made it necessary for US federal government to consider: whether programmes are narrowly focused enough on particular groups or economic sectors; whether race-neutral alternatives could be found (such as preferences based on wealth, income, family, education or geography); who suffered the burden of the particular programme; and whether they serve a 'compelling interest', that is a continuing need to combat discrimination. Here, detailed evidence of persisting racial discrimination in a specified sector is one of the important prerequisites for continuing with an action programme. The increasing number of lawsuits challenging affirmative action have been led by groups like Michael Greve's Centre for Individual Rights (www.cir-usa.org) who have played a key role in the gradual dismantling of widespread racial preference across many organisational contexts. The gradual tightening of restrictions on the permitted use of racial discrimination/preference in the USA brings affirmative action closer to the UK model of positive action. There is, however, a huge difference in the national debates with a mass of research, pro- and anti-campaigning groups, legal cases, organisational evidence and high-profile political discussion in the USA compared to a much quieter, and in some arenas silent, scene in the UK.

In order to establish the context for these case studies the construction of the concept of positive action in British race-relations law is provided. The news media in Britain has undergone a dramatic transformation in its coverage of race-related issues and minority groups in the last ten years. The extent to which this is attributable specifically to the impact of positive-action programmes, particularly those developed by the BBC, is examined here. The markedly uneven impact of positive-action strategies across newspapers, television and radio broadly correlates with the varying pattern of improvement in news media representation of race issues and minority groups. Although there are a complex of both conditional and determinate factors operating in both these examples, this evidence indicates the importance of renewing utilitarian arguments for positive-action strategies, through demonstrating the outcomes in terms of social utility and the wider enhancement of aggregate social welfare (Pitt, 1992).

Legal context and emerging initiatives

The first step to developing the legal concept of positive action in Britain was the recognition of key problems with the principle of non-discrimination. The White Paper on Racial Discrimination which introduced the Race Relations Act 1976 noted that, firstly, applying the principle of non-discrimination too strictly would 'actually impede the elimination of invidious discrimination and the encouragement of equal opportunity'. Secondly, attacks on discrimination were seen to be marginal if the absence of black and ethnic minority people in senior levels across virtually all occupations was not recognised (Home Office, 1975). As such, exceptions to non-discrimination were allowed in certain circumstances, and specific justification of such exceptions were set out as follows:

> Racial discrimination in the general provision of goods, services and job opportunities is unlawful but exception to this is permitted where,
>
> (i) no persons from a particular racial or ethnic group were doing particular work in an organisation in the last year;
> (ii) or, where there was 'underrepresentation' of that group in comparison to all those working in that organisation or in the relevant local labour market. (CRE, 1989)

Therefore, identifying a particular group or groups and gathering relevant data became a necessary first step for those groups or organisations seeking to both promote positive action and defend such action against challenge from those who were excluded from positive-action initiatives. Conceptual problems associated with this construction of positive action include difficulties with the categorisation of racial and ethnic groups, difficulties with measuring the extent of underrepresentation which hinge on the contested conceptualisation of equality (Turner, 1986), and the dubious assessment of the socioeconomic positions of black and minority ethnic groups against the 'white' norm, or the problem of standardising whiteness.

Despite these difficulties, many positive-action initiatives have involved the establishment of exclusive forms of vocational training with direct racial discrimination at the point of entry to these programmes, justified by data on underrepresentation. Given the conditions identified above, community and voluntary organisations, training bodies and private and public-sector employers may set up, and many have set up, training programmes exclusively for members of a particular racial or ethnic group designed to equip individuals to compete more effectively in the job market and progress into previously white-dominated employment sectors and on into middle and senior management. For example, in 1996 the Chief Executives of nine National Health Service Trusts in London approved the establishment of a 20-place positive-action training programme to address the issue of the low number of black and ethnic-minority managers. This programme began in October 1997 with an emphasis on the development of personal and management skills and competencies and the development of networking and support mechanisms to ensure a climate of encouragement and progression into higher management posts for those taking part. Such training programmes have proliferated and have been run by the BBC, major private-sector employers, local authorities and many others. They are slowly producing an increasing 'pool' of individuals who are gaining access to a range of managerial and professional fields. The number of such schemes is very small in comparison with the scale of labour-market inequalities and their impact has therefore been significant but marginal.

Other positive-action initiatives have included encouragement and outreach to particular groups to apply for jobs and services, targeted provision of services to meet special needs – for example sheltered housing schemes for African-Caribbean elderly or refuge provision for Asian women fleeing domestic violence – promotion of minority organisations and businesses through targeted grants, and advice on contract and grant compliance where increasing minority representation is tied to provision of government monies.

Beyond the issues of support for improved employment opportunities there is the broader question of opening doors into the policy and practice arena for organisations run by black minority ethnic people. This extends to capacity-building work with groups and organisations, effectively a collective parallel to the training offered for individuals (although it, too, may focus on key individuals). Within discourses about service provision this fits quite well with trends not explicitly related to ethnic divisions, concerned with user empowerment and participatory citizenship. Finally, we might consider access to the channels by which information is formed and distributed. Material for presentation in communications media could be sponsored or facilitated through positive-action strategies, and further spaces could be created directly for minority ethnic voices to be heard in the mainstream mass media. Judging from the historical record, the mass media would seem to offer a very appropriate terrain in which to develop positive-action strategies. This is because of underrepresentation in employment, lack of influence and voice in agenda-setting, and insensitivity, ignorance and prejudice in representation (in the other sense of the term) of minorities in media presentation of events. Interpreting positive action as a broad range of strategies, minority ethnic empowerment in this domain might be assisted by action focused on training, recruitment or promotion, on access to planning and production, on enhanced consultative and advisory networks, and on opening up spaces for more coverage of specific interests or activities. In fact all these could be linked, in that participation via employment might be a lever for increased sensitivity and better communications with minority communities.

Employment, training and institutional racism in the media

Employment of African-Caribbean and Asian journalists in the British media has significantly increased since the early 1980s due particularly to the development of positive-action training schemes and associated racial-equality strategies. In 1983, the Black Media Workers Association (BMWA) found that black workers comprised only 0.7 per cent of the total media workforce, with the proportion of black workers working full-time on newspapers and magazines at less than 0.2 per cent. The BMWA found only six black journalists working on provincial papers. In addition, a two-year survey of the principal journalists' training scheme found that only 0.04 per cent of the applicants were black (Gordon and Rosenberg, 1989). In her review of black-only journalism training courses, Ainley (1998: 50–5) identifies a series of initiatives beginning in 1983 with courses in London for 20 students in radio and print journalism, a Vauxhall College pre-entry newspaper journalism course for up to 30 students per year, and schemes run by the BBC from 1988 to 1994 in radio and television journalism for about 16 trainees per year.

According to a recent study (Ainley, 1998) there are approximately 12 to 20 black journalists out of a total of 3000 working on national newspapers (0.6%), and only 15 out of 8000 working on provincial newspapers (0.2%); whereas there are over 300 employed in radio and television broadcasting journalism, half of whom work in the black media. Fundamental racial and ethnic inequalities in employment in journalism in the British media remain. But, positive-action training schemes have successfully produced a pool of trained capable journalists many of whom have progressed and made a valuable contribution in news journalism. Most significantly this is one key factor in the improvement in coverage of race-related stories between 1985 and 1997 which is examined below, particularly where explicit decisions are made to use black journalists on such stories. This practice is confirmed by Ainley's recent study (1998: 57–82).

In response to the charge of institutional racism levelled at all major institutions in Britain by the report of the Stephen Lawrence Inquiry (February, 1999), Peter Preston the editor of the *Guardian* and Gary Younge, one of the few black journalists working on national newspapers, reflected on the record of response to these issues (*Guardian*, 1 March 1999 and Table 5.1). Peter Preston recognised both the need to employ more ethnic-minority reporters, editors and executives in the press and the long-term failure to do so. Preston identifes the Brixton

Table 5.1   Ethnic minority journalists on London-based national newspapers

Paper	Editors	Reporters	Columnists
Daily Mail	0	2	
Daily Telegraph	0	1	
Express / Sunday Express	3	3	
Financial Times	0	6	
Guardian	5	3	
Independent	1	3	1
Mirror	0	2	
Sun	0	1	
The Times	0	1	
Mail on Sunday	0	0	
News of the World	0	1	
Observer	0	2	
Sunday Mirror	0	0	
Sunday People	0	2	
Sunday Telegraph	0	1	
Sunday Times	1	3	
Total	10	31	1

Source: Gary Younge, *Guardian*, 1 March 1999.

riots as a key moment when he recognised the significance of this failure and 'how limited our antennae were'. After this he stresses the 'conspiracy' to hire ethnic-minority journalists, the shortage of 'high-flying candidates' and the competition for 'scarce talent'; this is, he sums up, a 'supply-side problem'. He also contrasts the rare and limited attempts at positive action in the UK with the 'vivid determination' of the *Guardian* in South Africa in recruiting and training black journalists.

In Europe, five media and training empowerment projects have been running since 1997 under the umbrella network of 'On Line/More Colour in the Media', involving partners in Sweden, the Netherlands, Greece, Germany and the UK. Research into minority ethnic employment in television was commissioned by this network (Ouaj, 1998; EIM, 1999) and this acknowledged the significance of positive action and related racial equality strategies in Britain which are far ahead of those in France, Germany and the Netherlands. The EIM report documented that ethnic minorities make up only 2–3 per cent of broadcasting workers across Europe compared to a population of about 8.5 per cent. A key objective here was to 'make cultural diversity part of the reality of television and radio' (Aitchison, 1999: 8). The five projects which have been established were set up at the Adolf-Grimme Institut in Germany, DIMITRA in Greece, the STOA (Stichting Omroep Allochtonen) Foundation in the Netherlands, Swedish Broadcasting and two projects in the UK. The British projects are New Visions: New Voices led by the London Film and Video Development Agency, and Intermedia led by Hammersmith and Fulham Borough. These projects contributed to change in a diverse set of ways: training qualified immigrant women (Germany), training and technical support for Greek-Russian journalistic trainees (Greece), development of multicultural programme ideas (Netherlands), securing explicit support for the promotion and reinforcement of cultural diversity in new media legislation (Sweden and Netherlands) and facilitation of pitching ethnic minority professionals' programme ideas to broadcasting companies (UK) (Aitchison, 1999: 15–16).

In Britain the BBC had an 8 per cent target for minority ethnic representation in 2000 amongst production, broadcast and news staff. In August 1997 the proportion for these three sectors was 6.3 per cent, 4.6 per cent and 7.1 per cent respectively. The part of the BBC with the lowest proportion of minority ethnic staff is in Northern Ireland

(0.7%), and recent research (Fawcett 1998) draws attention to persistent problems in coverage of race-related news in this region. The BBC's news service has the highest proportion of minority ethnic staff and here significant improvements in coverage have been identified. In France, positive-action strategies have generally been resisted; although there is evidence of renewed calls for action due to the exposure and persistence of endemic racism in broadcasting and a complete lack of black or North African newsreaders (*Guardian*, 16 December 1999).

In the UK, one interpretation of trends is that black minority participation has increased in such a way as to influence media orientations, cultural sensitivity, information networks, and output. If so (and the proposition would benefit from further empirical research), this would confirm the point established in other areas that there are important consequences arising from the roles played by black people (Law and Harrison, 1999), although in the media case this is within mainstream rather than separatist organisations (since the influence of black-run media channels remains limited by their specialised and small-scale character). Thus there may be 'ripple effects' from personnel changes, ranging from better organisational understanding of diverse cultures to the creation of role models.

This type of trend may reflect a variety of causative factors, including the increasing divergence of material conditions across ethnic groups, continuing pressure for change from minority ethnic organisations and activists (as well as staff), and more general shifts in socio-economic and political landscapes. It also reflects deliberate attempts from upper levels in the hierarchies of at least some organisations to promote change. As in other fields, there is a mixture of anti-racism and a concern for diverse constituencies.

The extent and nature of media responses, however, may be conditioned by market forces. In today's media environments there is certainly scope for developing more separate specialised and culturally-sensitive provision, but this – as with any interests outside the mass mainstreams – is subject to resources and market share being adequate. Future positive-action strategies might focus on resource allocation or on training and capacity-building for particular ethnic groups, but the former might be contentious as it could be interpreted as state support for the presentation of specific religious or cultural values.

Strategic difficulties

A distinctive characteristic of positive-action programmes is that they identify categories or groups, focus attention on group members, and may reach out to them or make specific arrangements for them, albeit often in the cause of creating a 'more-level playing field' for individuals or a more integrated society. The goal of altering institutional behaviour here may draw particularly on a justification founded in a perception of prior group exclusion or disadvantage. Specific strategies can lean towards assisting or training people in a framework orientated towards securing greater equality of *individualised* rights or chances, or can look towards more *collective* concepts of rights, emphasising collective 'special' or cultural needs, participation and voice, capacity building, role models, and so forth. To some extent these twin orientations or emphases have been exemplified by PATH and the Housing Corporation's strategies for minority ethnic housing associations, although with overlap between them. More generally, the two themes are related, share concerns and are not mutually exclusive. Invoking group disadvantage in a positive-action context, however, need not be unproblematic, even in the cause of greater equality of individual opportunity, and a focus on the collective needs or rights claims of groups can raise additional practical difficulties. Little detailed UK research has occurred on these matters, and the positive action political debate has not moved much beyond the assertion on the one hand that strategies are desirable to help marginalised groups, and on the other that interventions could interfere with 'fair' competition for jobs or resources. We will now explore some of the other issues in order to point to concerns that deserve more research as programmes develop under New Labour.

One problem concerns fragmentation and lack of homogeneity, whereby internal variation makes membership of a group a weak guide to the positions occupied by its individuals. Household and group identities are complex, and it is not straightforward to talk in terms of simple divides between black and white, disabled and able-bodied, or male and female. People have multiple identities and affiliations, and members of an identifiable group may occupy differing economic locations. Consequently, prioritising a group on the basis of its previous collective experiences of certain forms of oppression, exclusion or negative discrimination could be problematic, given the intersecting of the variables of class, gender, race, locality, ethnicity, disability, age and household structures. All members of a broad category (such as black minority ethnic people) may share negative consequences of (say) racism, but this tells us little on its own about the legitimacy of any group member's potential individual claim to priority over a member of another broad group. Ethnicity in itself certainly cannot serve as an unequivocal marker of disadvantage, and may indeed be a powerful source of strength for some communities (cf. Ballard, 1992).

A further potential area of difficulty concerns the privileging of particularisms and ethnicities. There might be a problem if positive-action strategies were cast in terms of a particular (relatively narrow) group's claim to management of resources, or to a share of jobs or promotions. Particularistic organisations can be exclusive at the expense of people who do not fit; their strength in catering for specified groups is also a weakness as far as outsiders or non-conformists are concerned (cf. Spicker, 1993/94; Harrison, 1995: 135–7). A historical example which resurfaces from time to time is the strategy of building a local 'community' within social rented housing by prioritising allocation of dwellings to friends and relatives of existing residents. Although at first glance apparently constructive, 'sons and daughters' policies of this kind have been racist in their intent and implementation, and have benefited whites. Yet housing practitioners might look favourably on a minority ethnic housing scheme where the presence of more than one family generation was encouraged so as to overcome the disadvantages older people experience because of a lack of English language skills. In employment, a particularistic organisation might take a strong line on employees; a denominational/religious school might be reluctant (for instance) to employ a single parent. There is a thus a political paradox, in that development of particularistic claims both strengthens demands for more fairness but also raises possibilities of new forms of exclusion. Furthermore, in the race-relations arena a focus on ethnic groups can point towards strategies of 'ethnic managerialism' in public policy, catering for and managing diversity, and giving rise to the suggestion that there has been a privileging of ethnicity in some respects (see Law, 1996: x–xi; and 1997b). This, too, is not necessarily unproblematic, although it can bring overdue benefits in terms of cultural sensitivity.

Managing implementation

Firstly, some kinds of positive action can be validated by reference to an organisation's own functional needs. A useful US example here is the emphasis placed on university mission statements which emphasise the value of diversity in teaching and learning environments as the key to validating affirmative action in university admissions. In certain instances a highly particular category of persons can be accorded priority in relation to a job or promotion because culturally-relevant skills or knowledge are required, or there may be something else that relates closely to work tasks. More generally, there may also be a case related to underrepresentation at the point of recruitment or within management, that can be important in relation to an organisation's needs to perform its general functions or connect with particular communities. The latter is clearly relevant in discussions of separatist organisational development – perhaps for some disabled people's organisations, gay or lesbian organisations, women's organisations or minority ethnic organisations – and it certainly seems legitimate that some agencies should focus on highly-specific groups. (This does not in itself, of course, imply anything about their rights to resources as against other organisations.) Within 'mainstream' services most of the concerns can be dealt with in the specifying of posts, and in training plans and capacity-building, although with care taken not to adopt essentialist stereotypes. It is sometimes easily defensible to identify a service or post primarily with a specific minority ethnic group, or with a client or service-user group.

A second way forward might be to adhere to and enlarge conventional equal-opportunities practices that can be applied across the board, and not to let a concept of 'fair shares' for groups displace a commitment to universalistic equality of status for individuals at points of access to jobs or resources, unless there is very sound and open justification. This is especially relevant for the employment sphere. Sometimes, broader changes will be necessary to help towards equal treatment for individuals, or to try to level the playing field. Here it is *change in environments* that will often be crucial, and some of the appropriate methods certainly fall under a positive-action heading. Actions can include alterations in the way training is offered, changes in the ways that posts are defined and remunerated, changes in accountability and participation, recognition of cultural diversity, taking minority needs into account when standards are set, and reaching out to include communities or categories of applicant or user that have previously been marginalised. Thus universalistic standards, practices and expectations may be renegotiated and recast, while remaining essential bases for equal opportunity.

A commitment to equality of status, of course, is not without limitations in its effects. Commitment to formally fair practices as they affect individuals is one reason why it has probably been more common in mainland Britain to proceed via training than to offer jobs as such to members of disadvantaged groups. The limitations of equality practices may encourage strategies focused on informal rather than formal methodologies, with people engaging with organisational politics in order to advance what they feel to be members' interests, adding their group's voices (when strong enough) to the existing networks of power and patronage. This should be viewed cautiously. There is no guarantee that those who succeed through such methods will manifest concerns for other disadvantaged groups, and there can be a thin divide between what seems like an essential strategy to change the distribution of employment or access to career ladders on the one hand, and oppressive tactics on the other.

A third way forward may be to accept a degree of particularism where it can be demonstrably seen as a corrective to continuing group marginalisation, and to construct mechanisms which facilitate the collective involvement of previously excluded groups in terms of voice and participation in policy networks or planning and production processes, representation of communities of interest, and opportunities to develop independent organisational capacities. As with the case built on functional needs noted above, this kind of positive action needs to rest on clear evidence. Given that the costs of positive-action policies may tend to be borne in the short term with the benefits accruing later (Stone, 1999: 10), early demonstration of useful results might be of particular importance. Strategy also needs to be conditioned by standard formal expectations about conformity to universalistic practices on equal opportunity. Meanwhile, it is important not to be mesmerised by assumptions about community representation into forgetting highly-individualised and multiple identities, and the fact that some people assumed to be part of a group will prefer other affiliations.

Conclusion

An indication that positive-action strategies aimed at intervening in patterns of institutional racism in news organisations are likely to become of increasing importance, particularly across Europe, was given in a recent piece on racism in France (CLUBLAND'S TRUE COLOURS, *Guardian*, 20 December 1999). Here, the launch of a pressure group of ethnic-minority media workers was reported, with the key aim of demanding 'positive discrimination' due to the 'endemic' racism in broadcasting. Also, in Belgium recent legislation has been passed which encourages the development of positive-action initiatives and political and social debate is growing over how to respond to this legal breakthrough.

In contrast, pessimistic lessons need to be learnt from the American experience (MINORITY HIRING GOALS RELEASED, Politico: the forum for Latino politics, 26 October 1998). Twenty years ago the American Society of Newspaper Editors (ASNE) set a goal for newsrooms across the country to reflect the racial and ethnic makeup of the communities they cover by the year 2000. According to the ASNE 1998 Newsroom Census, 11.46 per cent of newspaper journalists are from ethnic minorities compared to 26 per cent in the USA population whereas in 1978 these minorities accounted for less than 4 per cent of newsroom employees. So, despite some significant change there is still a huge gap in the representation of minorities here. The ASNE has now set 2025 as the year when this goal should be reached despite criticism of the distance of this goal by the National Association of Black Journalists. In examining the scale of change in minority airtime in American broadcasting, a study from the Southern Illinois University of the Big Three evening newscasts showed that minority journalists covered 15 per cent of stories in 1998, compared to 7 per cent in 1991 (MINORITIES GAIN AIR TIME, Politico, 19 February 1999). This study also reported that minority journalists made up 20 per cent of the 163-member network news staff. In the USA, therefore, despite major affirmative-action programmes which have shaped a 'river' of individual careers (Bowen and Bok, 1998; Leicht, 1999) and assisted in producing a large pool of talented minority journalists, it will take at least fifty years for newspapers to achieve minimum parity in the representation of minorities. Further work does need to be done across different national contexts to assess the linkages between changing patterns of minority staffing and changing patterns of news coverage of minority issues.

The issue of media representation of affirmative-action and positive-action debates is also critical here. In the USA, news coverage of this issue has been massive, engulfing programme managers and practitioners in a sea of political controversy. Frequent legal and legislative challenges have exposed the administration of affirmative-action programmes to great scrutiny. Yet, public support for affirmative action in the USA seems to have remained almost unchanged from 1965 to date, with over 70 per cent of whites supporting 'opportunity-enhancing' affirmative action together with opposition to quotas or 'preferential' policies (Entman and Rojecki, 2000: 112–3). This brings American public opinion close to the British legal position and these views on 'tighter' policy are now reflected in US White House policy. The attempts by the news media to talk up and misrepresent public opinion on affirmative action as a fundamental clash of interests between white and black in the 1990s and beyond has proved to be out of step with the American electorate. In the 1996 and 2000 elections, the affirmative-action issue proved to be a low priority for voters. Bush's public statements about supporting 'affirmative access', however hollow, presented some sort of consensus with Gore and this issue drew little news coverage in the 2000 election. The future of affirmative action was up for voters to decide in Florida, but subsequent events completely obliterated the outcome of this particular decision from the news.

A diametrically-opposite picture of news coverage emerges in the UK. In the main, little if any attention is given to coverage of positive action. News items generally restrict themselves to reporting new initiatives rather than presenting an explosive clash of racial interests. A recent piece, 'FAST TRACK' PLAN TO PROMOTE BLACK AND ASIAN POLICE (*Observer*, 29 October 2000) illustrates this process. Here, a controversy over whether American-style preference policies should be introduced in the police service sets up the debate in a different form. A University academic supporting preference is shown in conflict with the Conservative Shadow Home Secretary over this issue with the government position presented as one of 'extensive' but 'ineffective' action over racial inequality in police employment. The Home Office spokeswoman finally douses the debate, declaring affirmative action illegal in Britain.

This chapter has focused on recent historical experiences in order to review 'what works', and has considered some issues for practitioners. The ethical debates about compensation for past disadvantages have not been addressed here, but the powerful argument that positive action is necessary in the interests of developing a more stable and open society, and reducing social divides that threaten everyone's safety has been proposed. The priority of particular notions of rights also lies outside this discussion, but it has been established that rights claims may clash, and that assertions of group rights are highly contestable. It is certainly easier to talk of the right of all groups to inhabit an environment free of the racial harassment (or hostile media coverage) that no-one should have to experience, than to talk in terms of specific groups having distinct rights claims that should be met through mechanisms such as quotas, 'fast-tracking', or media exposure. Indeed, part of this discussion has stressed tensions implicit in the group or category basis that underpins positive-action strategies.

Despite the reservations, positive or affirmative action seems to be working well. Analysis of selected positive-action strategies indicated successes from the point of view of voice and participation, role models, and anti-racism and cultural sensitivity in service delivery. Changes in mainstream media, where personnel changes may be viewed alongside changes in treatment of news and other materials, has also been identified. Positive-action strategies in general may have effects not only for recruitment and the delivery of services, but also in the climate for discussion and practice. *Discourses* linked with the provision of services and resources have been affected significantly, although of course other causative factors have been operating as well. It is no surprise – after more than a decade of separatist organisational development – that a New Labour minister has referred to the need for services to be 'culturally competent and inclusive' (Housing Corporation, 1998: 1). The citizen as consumer of services – or as a subject for media stories – is recognised as a more varied person than hitherto, but this variety is no longer seen as such a legitimate basis for pejorative racist identification.

There are bound to be qualifications about the extent to which change has lasting effects. In the media, moral panics or pressures of international events may still shift debates against the fair presentation of specific groups (whether 'travellers' or asylum-seekers). In UK society generally, the ideal of a level playing field may still be more of a dream than an achieved reality.

Lastly, it is important to emphasise the continuing significance of universalistic principles as applied traditionally in conventional equal-opportunities policies. Goals like cultural sensitivity will be less vulnerable to political challenge if they are fitted into a general framework of equalities of status that is implicitly multicultural, while accommodating diversities of affiliation and choice may well be easiest within an overall framework of universalistic rights and resources (cf. Harrison, 1995: 145–6). In the employment sphere one ideal would appear to be to *adjust organisational environments* so that minority ethnic citizens have fewer obstacles to face, and to take account of diversity, but without abandoning the drive for formal equality of status amongst all persons that has been such a hard-fought goal of earlier struggles. For individuals the traditional equal-opportunities agenda of formal fairness on a case-by-case basis remains very important. Going beyond this in the interests of a wider group may be desirable, but requires caution and sound methodologies. There can be tensions between group and individual rights claims; apparently reducing the rights of some people by advancing others could be a high-risk approach; the justification must be absolutely clear. There is an urgent need to renew efforts to improve minority representation in news organisations at all levels precisely because of the linkage to improved patterns of coverage of minority issues, and also the more positive perceptions of news output and news organisations by minority audiences themselves. In changing patterns of staffing, positive-action strategies and initiatives are of vital importance and strong organisational leadership is the key to success.

Conclusion

Racism and anti-racism are powerful twin social forces that will continue to shape news communications through the twenty-first century. They operate in many different ways across differing national and international contexts, and there is still much work to be done to map this complicated terrain. Trans-nationally, global news communications are a rapidly-changing environment where representations of race are subject to dynamic movement, with old images and messages continually being rehearsed and reshaped in conjunction with the production of new images and messages of both inclusion and exclusion. Examination of the proliferation and variety of these racialised themes and messages in both British and American news has been a key focus here, with ample evidence to show that race remains a strong binding thread in many news stories. Globally, the news media play a key role in both challenging established identities and related world-views, and in initiating and transmitting ideas and images which influence and shape new world-views (Gabriel, 1998: 187). Yet the forces of migration, ethnicity and racism also remain powerful, continuing to inspire conflict and war, seemingly untouched by the new power of global communications.

Summary of key themes

The task set out in Chapter 1 was to address issues of the conceptualisation and measurement of racism and debates over how to assess racism in the media. This may seem too intellectual for some, a task to be dismissed as irrelevant when racism is so glaringly obvious. Yet, to engage and seek to challenge and undermine racism requires attention to the complex chameleon-like character of racism, which is subject to variation and change in form and content across contexts and times. Given this complexity it is useful to identify those elements that are universal. In Chapter 1, six key universal elements of racism were identified. These were the signification of race characteristics to identify a collectivity; the attribution of such a group with negative bio-

157

logical or cultural characteristics; the designation of boundaries to specify inclusion and exclusion; variation in form in that it may be a relatively coherent theory or a loose assembly of images and explanations; its practical adequacy (in that it successfully 'makes sense' of the world for those who articulate it); and lastly its pleasures ('an unearned easy feeling of superiority and the facile cementing of group identity on the fragile basis of arbitrary antipathy'). Taking the first two key elements, put more simply, *racism involves the signification of race to define a collectivity, which is then referred to negatively*. To measure racism in the media, specification is therefore required of these two elements, the extent and nature of the signification of race and an evaluation of forms and mechanisms of negative attribution.

In examining the conceptual tools available from earlier studies to measure negative racial attribution in the media, four methods were found to predominate. These involved either measurement of the negative attribution of minorities in relation to whiteness, assessment of racial and cultural representation in comparison to 'real' life, evaluation of the privileging and silencing of different cultural voices in relation to Eurocentric norms, and, privileging the perceptions of negative attribution held by racialised groups themselves.

The power of interrogating hegemonic whiteness and its symbolic sense of moral and aesthetic superiority was found to be a much stronger form of critique than that of 'standardising whiteness', that is comparing the representation of minorities against a white norm. The power of claims for 'progressive realism' was seen in the ways in which this had inspired many examples of passionate protest over distorted media representation by minority groups. The critical task of pinpointing the different 'cultural voices at play and those drowned out' in media texts was seen to be valuable in foregrounding questions of the omissions and silences in patterns of representation. The value of privileging the voices of minorities themselves in assessment of media output was seen as particularly important because of the gulf in knowledge, of the detail of everyday life in minority ethnic households and communities, between white media practitioners and minority audiences. Lastly, data on minority perceptions of news output was seen to show that many from African-Caribbean and Asian communities felt that these organisations failed to provide an adequate news service for them.

Minority ethnic perceptions of news content fitted closely with the definition of institutional racism used in the Stephen Lawrence

Inquiry, these included perceptions of racial and ethnic bias against them, an inappropriate service for people from differing cultural and ethnic groups, and prejudice, ignorance, thoughtlessness and racist stereotyping which disadvantages minority ethnic people.

In examining news content it was argued that there is no necessary correspondence between racist news items and audience racism; racist messages may or may not, therefore, be appropriated or even recognised by the consumer. Therefore, some, particularly white news consumers, may be totally oblivious to the forms of racism encapsulated in a news item, others may appropriate a racist message and convert it into part of their everyday world, while others may recognise such items and reject the message. The variation in patterns of audience reception, and in producer intentions, does not undermine *the importance and significance of the 'autonomous' task of analysing, identifying and challenging the way in which racialised individuals and groups are constructed in the news.* The wealth of critical tools available for this task informed a major empirical study, which was presented in Chapter 2.

Daily coverage of race news on television, radio and in the broadsheet and tabloid press was analysed over a six-month period (November 1996 to May 1997) and this showed *a significant shift in coverage between the 1980s and the 1990s, moving from overt hostility to anti-racism towards the presentation of an 'anti-racist show'.* It was argued that this 'great anti-racist show' may, in some news organisations, be operating as an outward, empty attempt of mere display masking continuing normative and progressive whiteness in news organisations, racial and ethnic inequalities of power and employment and a collective failure to provide appropriate quality news services for black and minority ethnic communities and consumers. Such a 'show' may well, therefore, be playing against a backcloth of institutional racism. Nevertheless, in the case study of British news, just under *three-quarters of news items studied presented a broadly anti-racist message,* including items which sought to expose and criticise racist attitudes, statements, actions and policies, which addressed the concerns of immigrant and minority ethnic groups and showed their contribution to British society, and which embraced an inclusive view of multicultural British identity. There are a complex of factors which account for this process including changing cultural, political and government discourse over race issues, changes in minority ethnic employment profiles in some news organisations, increasing recognition of anti-racism and multiculturalism in regulatory environments, and competitive rivalry in news production. The balance between pro-minority and anti-minority messages varied across news media, with television news carrying the highest proportion of anti-racist messages (83%) and the tabloids carrying the smallest proportion (66%). There was also, in the press, a pattern of decline in the quantity of race-related items since the mid-1980s, despite the coverage of the Stephen Lawrence Inquiry. This may indicate a lessening of the 'race-relations' frame in British news coverage and a reduction in the coverage of minority ethnic affairs and migration. The 'fit' between race news selected by editors and the real pattern of race-related newsworthy events is, as with other types of news, likely to be poor. The largest thematic category of race news contained stories relating to crime and violence, with little proportional thematic difference across television, radio and the tabloids. In addition, immigration was more likely to be treated in a sympathetic and humanitarian fashion, the press silence on black people as victims of violence was found to no longer exist, multiculturalism and Islam were more likely to be valued than vilified in news items, and there was little coverage seeking to deny the existence of racism.

The growing strength of broadly anti-racist news values goes hand in hand with a significant core group of news messages which foster racism, animosity and hatred. In the British case study, about a quarter of news items conveyed a negative message about minority groups. The daily repetition of linkages between race, violence, dangerousness and crime is a constant feature of news in general. Also, key 'old' news frames, or traditional racist messages, persist; that is, the presentation of selective groups of citizens and migrants as a welfare burden who are prone to deception, fraud and other forms of crime and, hence, racialised forms of social control are justified including race-driven forms of policing and discriminatory forms of immigration control. By these means black, Asian and other migrant groups are constructed as a social problem in a range of ways, often with little attention to real social welfare issues amongst those communities – for example homelessness, poor housing conditions, poor educational opportunities and restricted provision of health services and social welfare.

Reporting on migration issues was found to be a continuing source of racial hostility. This has been frequently led by government sources with concern expressed over abuse, fraud and deceit and other forms of illegal activity. News coverage of this issue has been shown to be often characterised by sloppy journalism with little attention to the real costs and benefits of complex migration flows. In these ways the news media, particularly the press, selectively repeat, rework and reinvent a simple pattern of key racist messages which have 'helped to build a respectable, coherent, common-sense whiteness' (Gabriel, 1998: 188). In addition, the crucial 'steering' role of the major political parties, and in particular government leadership, on these issues was established as central to the rise and fall of media hostility to racialised migrant groups.

The assessment of bias in news reporting was found to be a complex affair involving a range of strategies to evaluate news presentation, selection, balance and impartiality (Gunter, 1997). Editorial bias in selection of race items was indicated in Chapter 2 by the identification of differing news agendas across different news media.

An evaluation of more deliberate racial bias in British news content confirmed the evidence of significant progress and improvement in reporting race issues in the news media in comparison to the 1980s.

Overall, most items were found to be neutral with more evidence that journalists were prepared to advocate on behalf of minorities than express deliberate hostility towards them. In Northern Ireland, a study of newspapers showed that these encouraging trends were not in evidence. Minority ethnic groups' concerns were largely marginalised in the news reflecting weak political leadership, poor journalistic professionalism and unconscious racism.

Labels and names for particular groups carry particular and changing ideological baggage. Use of categories and terminology requires sensitivity to the people concerned. The British news media operate in a confused position often retaining spurious racial categories and using ethnicity with little understanding. Black people are still twice as likely to be racially described as such than white people in news items, and in many cases this is unnecessary. Overall, race thinking pervades news coverage of migrants and ethnic relations and the thoroughly mistaken notion that races are real is continually reinforced.

The 'great anti-racist show' is live and kicking in British news, and, as with many forms of entertainment, tried and tested formulas prevail. News organisations and journalists do seem to be working within previously established discursive conventions of what anti-racism should be about, as opposed to elevating the 'unexpected' and pushing forward the serious debate over how to fundamentally shift British racism. Anti-racist rhetoric is strong, and exposing the stupidity of racism does make front-page news. Here, there is a recurring tendency to refer to the racist comments of public figures as 'gaffes', with in-grained racism thus reduced to the status of an unconscious indiscreet blunder. Further, it is such 'unwitting stereotyping' that was shown to be the driving force for systematic institutional racism in the Lawrence Inquiry. Nevertheless, it is better to see racism ridiculed in the news than anti-racism. There is a virtual silence about the 'stupidity' and 'lunacy' of anti-racism policies and initiatives in the late 1990s. The dominant news frame in the 1980s has gone and this does indicate the extent to which anti-racist discourse has permeated news organisations and may now be a more 'normal' news value itself.

As yet, the further shift in race news forwards (or backwards) to an increasing focus on the problems of white individuals and groups 'spoken through the language of racism' (Mac an Ghaill, 1999) has not taken place. The plight of white victims of racism has been high-lighted in news stories, but these remain infrequent in comparison to the volume of coverage dealing with minority ethnic victims of racism. This pattern may quickly change with new angles and images used to move beyond conventional approaches to race issues in news reporting, particularly given the volatile, ambivalent and fickle charac-ter of this 'anti-racist show'. A simple retreat from this position also seems to regularly occur in some sections of some news media where it becomes fashionable again to pour vitriol on attempts to challenge racism, and where backward-looking forms of cultural affirmation are used to provide strong, entirely 'sensible' justifications for advocating racial and cultural purity and hostility to those outside the white nation.

The Stephen Lawrence story dominated the news items examined during this study and was described as the *'biggest sea change in media coverage of race'*, by Michael Mansfield QC, (*Media Guardian*, 19 April 1999; emphasis added). He notes the indifference of news organisations and current affairs programmes to the case early on (1993/94) compared to the extensive news, documentary and drama coverage more recently. Also, in relation to race crime more generally he recognised significant improvements in both local and national coverage. What this sea change will bring next in terms of trends in race news is uncertain and unknown. At best we can expect courage, innovation and creativity in identifying institutional racism and forms of racial, ethnic and cultural exclusion. In Britain the overall picture of institutional racism that emerged from news coverage highlighted the immigration service, criminal justice organisations, football clubs, health authorities and trusts, the armed forces and private employers like Fords as key problem areas. There is no silence here about the range and diversity of institutional racism and racism is not simply reduced to the problem of racist individuals as some critics have suggested (Gordon and Rosenberg, 1989). The improved news coverage of anti-racist campaigning activity is a key change since the 1980s which reflects an increased openness to minority voices. British news and documentary-making contains a powerful thread of output that does excel in carrying these messages and debates forward. The renewal of confidence in anti-racist voices together with strong anti-racist political leadership may further strengthen and deepen this process across the news media.

In America, the development of an 'anti-racist show' in news content does seem to be a weaker trend than in the UK, and there is a need for further research here. Recent research highlights the dominance of ongoing problems in the portrayal of blacks and whites and little in the way of effective anti-racist journalism (Entman and Rojecki, 2000). However, recently selected items were used in Chapter 4 to indicate the changing shape and style of anti-racism in US news. Here again the significance of political leadership is a key factor. There were strong parallels in political positions taken in elections in the UK in 1997 and in the USA in 2000. Talking-up ethnic diversity and the significance of the non-white vote and keeping silent on issues of immigration were marked features of this cross-party consensus. The fragility of this consensus in the UK has been shown in recent political and social conflict over new patterns of migration, and this is also a likely scenario in the USA. One outcome of changing patterns of racism in both Europe and America has been hostility to positive strategies to tackle racial and ethnic inequalities. There is some evidence that debates over positive-action are diverging. Renewal of interest, support for and innovation in positive-action strategies across some European countries, and also particularly in South Africa, is increasingly contrasting with the decline in and dismantling of affirmative-action strategies in the USA. Nevertheless, there has been significant progress in achieving change in minority representation in media organisations in the USA due partly to the impact of these strategies, as employment of minority ethnic journalists on American newspapers increased from 4 per cent to 11 per cent between 1978 and 1998. The picture, particularly amongst newspapers, is much more grim in Britain where there has been a much smaller investment and effort in positive-action strategies which seek to shift white dominance in employment and this was examined in Chapter 5.

There has been a *general lack of attention to the underrepresentation of minority ethnic groups in the British news media.* Ainley (1998) has identified that there are approximately 12 to 20 black journalists out of a total of 3000 working on national newspapers (0.6%), and only 15 out of 8000 working on provincial newspapers (0.2%); whereas there are over 300 black people employed in radio and television broadcasting journalism, half of whom work in the black-led media. But, positive-action training schemes have successfully produced a pool of trained capable journalists many of whom have progressed and made a valuable contribution in news journalism. Most significantly this is one key factor in the improvement in coverage of race-related stories between 1985 and 1997, particularly where explicit decisions have been made to use minority journalists on such stories. However, such decisions have also involved using minority journalists in the coverage of hostile 'anti-minority' stories. There is an urgent need to renew efforts to improve minority representation in news organisations and amongst government communications staff at all levels, precisely because of the linkage to improved patterns of coverage of minority issues. In addition, more positive perceptions of news and communications output and news organisations by multicultural audiences themselves are likely to be created as a result of such action. In changing patterns of staffing, positive-action strategies and initiatives are of vital import-ance, and strong organisational and government leadership is the key to change. However, change is likely to be slow, and racial and ethnic inequalities will remain for many decades to come in both the UK and the USA.

Institutional racism in news organisations

In the absence of adequate representation of minority ethnic groups in major news organisations, particularly at senior levels, readers, listen-ers and viewers from those groups will probably continue to remain concerned about racial and ethnic bias in the production of news and dissatisfied with the quality and appropriateness of news services for them. This study has shown that despite these patterns of inequality, news output has undergone a significant transformation in its coverage of minority ethnic affairs and migration.

Nevertheless, the persistence of a significant core of hostile racist news messages and the failure of legal and regulatory action to provide an effective response to these problems warrants more comprehensive action. Many social institutions in the UK, including the armed forces, have been subject to thorough investigation of institutional racism; news organisations have not. Given the evidence presented here, it is proposed that, a National Inquiry into Institutional Racism in the British News Media be established. Irrespective of whether this call for an Inquiry is heeded, technological and regulatory changes are increasingly producing an environment that facilitates rapid changes in news organisations and their output. Media-industry fragmentation, flexible working practices and changing relationships between news producers and their multicultural audiences are producing great opportunities for improving the provision of appropriate and professional news services. In this context, it is realistic to place a burden of expectation on major news organisations that coverage should continue to show a trend of improvement. Going with the grain of dominant trends in news coverage through the 1990s, this would mean:

- extending the news coverage of various forms of racism, racial violence, racial discrimination, persistent forms of white privilege and initiatives to tackle racism and promote ethnic equality and cultural diversity;
- producing more news that highlights the contribution of minority ethnic groups and migrant groups to British society, not just individuals in entertainment and sport;
- providing more informed news coverage about migration, which promotes better understanding of the benefits and complexities of migrant flows;
- promoting debate and public understanding about the ethnic and cultural diversity of those people both living in Britain and abroad;
- eradicating the deliberate shaping of news items that show, present or promote hostility to minority ethnic groups;
- increasing precision and accuracy and attention to relevance and social identity in identifying the ethnic origin of groups and individuals;

- developing an extended range of positive-action initiatives and innovations to improve ethnic minority representation in news organisations;
- ensuring explicit attention to issues of anti-racism and ethnic diversity in legislative, regulatory and policy environments in which news organisations operate;
- abandoning old/traditional race-relations and immigration frames in presenting news events and finding new ways to present issues of social diversity, division and difference.

A new context of declining media, political and social hostility to both settled minority ethnic groups and new migrant groups can provide the conditions for the creation of a climate of greater trust in which more open discussion and debate of sensitive issues affecting minority ethnic groups in the news can fruitfully take place. These more progressive social spaces are continually subject to the swift remembering, reinvention and restatement of hostile messages, as seen in the UK in the first years of this century. The strength of white backlash culture (Gabriel, 1998) must never be underestimated, and the strength of repeated linkages between violence, crime, race and migration remain the most worrying aspects of contemporary news coverage.

References

Ainley, B. (1995) *Blacks and Asians in the British Media*, unpublished summary.

Ainley, B. (1998) *Black Journalists, White Media* (Stoke-on-Trent: Trentham).

Aitchison, C. (1999) *Tuning in to Diversity, a handbook for promoting more diversity in the media*, Utrecht: On Line / More Colour in the Media.

Alibhai-Brown, Y. (1998) 'The Media and Race Relations', in T. Blackstone, B. Parekh and P. Sanders (eds), *Race Relations in Britain, a Developing Agenda* (London: Routledge).

Alibhai-Brown, Y. (1999) *True Colours, Public Attitudes to Multiculturalism and the Role of the Government* (London: Institute for Public Policy Research).

Aldrich, L. S. (1999) *Covering the Community: A Diversity Handbook for Media* (London: Sage).

Anwar, M. and Shang, A. (1982) *Television in a Multi-Racial Society* (London: Commission for Racial Equality).

BBC Broadcasting Research (1996) *Ethnic Listening in the UK* (London: BBC).

Ballard, R. (1992) 'New clothes for the Emperor? The Conceptual Nakedness of the Race Relations Industry in Britain', *New Community*, vol. 18, no. 3, April, pp. 481–92.

Banton, M. (1970) 'The Concept of Racism', in S. Zubaida (ed.), *Race and Racialism* (London: Tavistock).

Barry, A. (1988) 'Black Mythologies: Representation of Black People on British Television', in J. Twitchin (ed.), *The Black and White Media Show* (Stoke-on-Trent: Trentham).

Benewick, R. (1972) *The Fascist Movement in Britain* (London: Allen Lane, Penguin).

Benjamin, I. (1995) *The Black Press in Britain* (Stoke on Trent: Trentham).

Ben-Tovim, G., Brown, V., Clay, D., Law, I., Lay, L. and Torkington, P. (1980) *Racial Disadvantage in Liverpool* (Liverpool: Merseyside Area Profile Group).

Berry, V. T. and Manning-Miller, C. L. (eds) (1996) *Mediated Messages and African-American Culture* (London: Sage).

Bonnett, A. (1993) *Radicalism, Anti-Racism and Representation* (London: Routledge).

Bowen, W.G. and Bok, D. (1998) *The Shape of the River* (New Jersey: Princeton University Press).

Bourne, S. (1998) *Blacks in the British Frame* (London: Cassell).

Brown, R. (1965) *Social Psychology* (London: Macmillan – now Palgrave).

168 *References*

Calves, G. and Sabbagh, D. (1999) 'Affirmative Action in Contemporary France: A Challenge to Citizenship', in M. Martinelli and T. Judt (eds), *The Politics of Affirmative Action and the Development of Multi-cultural Citizenship: Euro–US Perspectives* (New York: Remarque Institute, New York University).

Campbell, C. (1995) *Race, Myth and News* (London: Sage).

Centre for Integration and Improvement of Journalism (CIIJ) (1994) *News Watch: A Critical Look at Coverage of People of Colour* (San Francisco: San Francisco State University).

Chow, K. (1997) 'Imagining Boundaries of Blood: Zhang Binglin and the Invention of the "Han" Race in Modern China', in F. Dikotter (ed.), *The Construction of Racial Identities in China and Japan* (London: Hurst).

Clegg, J. (1994) *Fu Manchu and the 'Yellow Peril': The Making of a Racist Myth* (Stoke-on-Trent: Trentham).

Collins, R. and Murroni, C. (1996) *New Media, New Policies* (Cambridge: Polity Press).

Commission for Racial Equality (1989) *Positive Action in Housing* (London: CRE).

Cottle, S. (1992) ' "Race", Racialization and the Media: A Review and Update of Research', *Sage Race Relations Abstracts*, vol. 17, no. 2, pp. 3–57.

Cottle, S. (1997) *Television and Ethnic Minorities: Producers' Perspectives* (Aldershot: Avebury).

Cottle, S. (1999) 'Ethnic Minorities and the British News Media: Explaining (Mis) Representation', in J. Stokes and A. Reading (eds), *The Media in Britain, Current Debates and Developments* (London: Macmillan – now Palgrave).

Critcher, C., Parker, M. and Sondhi, R. (1975) *Race in the Provincial Press* (Birmingham: Centre for Contemporary Cultural Studies).

Cummerbatch, G. and Woods, S. with Stephenson, C., Boyle, M., Smith, A. and Gauntlett, S. (1996) *Ethnic Minorities on Television* (London: Independent Television Commission).

Curtis, L. (1971) *Apes and Angels: The Irishmen in Victorian Caricature* (Newton Abbot: David & Charles).

Daniels, T. (1990) 'Beyond Negative and Positive Images', in J. Willis and T. Wollen (eds), *The Neglected Audience* (London: British Film Institute).

Daniels, T. and Gerson, J. (eds) (1989) *The Colour Black* (London: BFI Publishing).

Delano, A. and Henningham, J. (1995) *The News Breed: British journalism in the 1990s* (London: London Institute).

Dennis, E. and Pease, E. (eds) (1997) *The Media in Black and White* (New Brunswick: Transaction).

Dickens, C. (1861) *The Uncommercial Traveller* (London: Oldham Press).

van Dijk, T. (1991) *Racism in the Press* (London: Routledge).

van Dijk, T. (1993) *Elite Discourse and Racism* (London: Sage).

Dikotter, F. (ed.) (1997) *The Construction of Racial Identities in China and Japan* (London: Hurst).

Dines, G. and Humez, J. (eds) (1995) *Gender, Race and Class in the Media* (London: Sage).

Dyer, R. (1997) *White* (London: Routledge).

Edwards, J. (1995) *The Morality of Racial Preference in Britain and America* (London: Routledge).

Entman, R. M. and Rojecki, A. (2000) *The Black Image in the White Mind, Media and Race in America* (Chicago: University of Chicago Press).

Essed, P. (1991) *Understanding Everyday Racism* (London: Sage).

European Institute for the Media (1999) *Employment and Access of Ethnic Minorities to the Television Industry in Germany, United Kingdom, France, the Netherlands and Finland* (Dusseldorf: European Institute for the Media).

Fanon, F. (1967) *The Wretched of the Earth* (Harmondsworth: Penguin).

Fawcett, L. (1998) 'Fitting in: Ethnic Minorities and the News Media', in P. Hainsworth (ed.), *Divided Society, Ethnic Minorities and Racism in Northern Ireland* (London: Pluto).

Ferguson, R. (1998) *Representing 'Race': Ideology and Identity in the Media* (London: Arnold).

Fiske, J. (1996) *Media Matters* (London: Routledge).

Fiske, J. and Hartley, J. (1978) *Reading Television* (London: Routledge).

Foucault, M. (1980) *Power/Knowledge* (Brighton: Harvester).

Fowler, R. (1991) *Language in the News* (London: Routledge).

Frachon, C. and Vargaftig, M. (ed.) (1995) *European Television: Immigrants and Ethnic Minorities* (London: John Libbey).

Frankenberg, R. (1993) *The Social Construction of Whiteness: White Women, Race Matters* (London: Routledge).

Gabriel, J. (1998) *Whitewash, Racialised Politics and the Media* (London: Routledge).

Gandy, O. H. Jr (1998) *Communication and Race: a Structural Perspective* (London: Arnold).

Gillborn, D. (1995) *Racism and Anti-Racism in Real Schools* (Buckingham: Open University Press).

Gillespie, M. (1995) *Television, Ethnicity and Cultural Change* (London: Routledge).

Gilligan, C. (1982) *In a Different Voice* (Cambridge, MA: Harvard University).

van Ginneken, J. (1998) *Understanding Global News* (London: Sage).

Gilroy, P. (1990) 'The end of anti-racism', in W. Ball and J. Solomos (eds), *Race and Local Politics* (London: Macmillan – now Palgrave).

Glasgow Media Group (1997a) *'Race', Migration and Media* (Glasgow: GMG).

Glasgow Media Group (1997b) *'Race' and the Public Face of Television* (Glasgow: GMG).

Glasgow Media Group (1997c) *Ethnic Minorities in Television Advertising* (Glasgow: GMG).

Goldberg, D.T. (1993) *Racist Culture: Philosophy and the Culture of Meaning* (Oxford: Blackwell).

Gonzalez, P. and Rodriguez, R. (1999) *Television Brownout Protests Further Whitening of Media* (www.minorities-jb.com/african/civil/brownout0913.htm).

Gordon, P. (1987) 'Visas and the British Press', *Race and Class*, vol. 28 (3), Winter.

Gordon, P. and Rosenberg, D. (1989) *Daily Racism* (London: Runnymede Trust).

Guillaumin, C. (1995) *Racism, Sexism, Power and Ideology* (London: Routledge).

Gunter, B. (1997) *Measuring Bias on Television* (Luton: John Libbey).

Gunter, B., Fazal, S. and Wober, M. (1991) *Ethnic Minority Attitudes to Broadcasting Issues* (London: Independent Television Commission).

Hall, S. (1981) 'The Whites of Their Eyes: Racist Ideologies and the Media', in G. Bridges and R. Brunt (eds), *Silver Linings: Some Strategies for the Eighties* (London: Lawrence & Wishart).

Hall, S. (1992) 'The Question of Cultural Identity', in S. Hall, D. Held and T. McGrew, *Modernity and its Futures* (London: Sage/Open University).

Hall, S. (1995) 'Black and White in television', in J. Givanni (ed.), *Remote Control* (London: British Film Institute).

Hall, S. (1997a) 'The Centrality of Culture: Notes on the Cultural Revolutions of our Time', in K. Thompson (ed.), *Media and Cultural Regulation* (London: Sage/Open University).

Hall, S. (ed.) (1997b) *Representation: Cultural Representations and Signifying Practices* (London: Sage/Open University).

Hall, S. and Jacques, M. (1997) 'Les enfants de Marx and Coca-Cola', *New Statesman*, 28 November, pp. 34–6.

Hall, S., Critcher, C., Jefferson, T., Clarke, J. and Roberts, B. (1978) *Policing the Crisis: Mugging, the State and Law and Order* (London: Macmillan – now Palgrave).

Harrison, M. (1995) *Housing, 'Race', Social Policy and Empowerment* (Aldershot: Avebury).

Hartmann, P. and Husband, C. (1974) *Racism and the Mass Media* (London: Davis Poynter).

Hepple, B. and Szyszczak, E. (eds) (1992) *Discrimination: the Limits of Law* (London: Mansell).

Hetherington, A. (1985) *News, Newspapers and Television* (London: Macmillan – now Palgrave).

Hikins, H.R. (ed.) (1973) *Building the Union* (Liverpool: Toulouse Press).

Holland, P. (1981) 'The New Cross Fire and the Popular Press', *Multi-Racial Education*, vol. 9(3), pp. 61–80.

Home Office (1975) *Racial Discrimination*, Cmnd 6234 (London: HMSO).

Home Office (1999) *The Stephen Lawrence Inquiry*, Cm 4262–I (London: Stationery Office).

References

171

Housing Corporation (1998) *Black and Minority Ethnic Housing Policy* (London: The Housing Corporation).

Husband, C. (1974) 'Responsible Journalism for a Multi-Racial Britain', *New Community*, vol. 4 (1).

Husband, C. (ed.) (1994) *A Richer Vision: the Development of Ethnic Minority Media in Western Democracies* (Paris/London: UNESCO/John Libbey).

Hylton, C. (1998) *African-Caribbean Community Organisations* (Stoke-on-Trent: Trentham).

Independent Television Commission (1996) *Television: Ethnic Minorities' Views* (London: ITC).

Iyengar, S. and Reeves, R. (eds) (1997) *Do the Media Govern? Politicians, Voters and Reporters in America* (London: Sage).

Jakubowicz, A. (ed.) (1994) *Racism, Ethnicity and the Media* (Sydney: Allen & Unwin).

Jay, P. and Birt, J. (1975) 'Can Television News Break the Understanding Barrier?' *The Times*, 28 February.

Johnson, P.B. and Sears, D.O. (1971) 'Black Invisibility, the Press and the Los Angeles Riot', *American Journal of Sociology*, vol. 76(1), pp. 698–721.

Jones, T. (1993) *Britain's Ethnic Minorities* (London: Policy Studies Institute).

Joppke, C. (1999) 'Affirmative Action and Multicultural Citizenship in Germany', in M. Martinelli and T. Judt (eds), *The Politics of Affirmative Action and the Development of Multi-cultural Citizenship: Euro–US perspectives* (New York: Remarque Institute, New York University).

Law, I. (1996) *Racism, Ethnicity and Social Policy* (Hemel Hempstead: Harvester Wheatsheaf).

Law, I. (1997a) 'Race', *Historical Journal of Film, Radio and Television*, Special Issue: *The Battle for Britain, Political Broadcasting and the British Election of 1997*, vol. 17 (4), October, pp. 485–9.

Law, I. (1997b) 'Modernity, Anti-Racism and Ethnic Managerialism', *Policy Studies*, vol. 18 (3 / 4), pp. 189–206.

Law, I. (1999) 'Positive Action and its Impact on Community Participation in Housing and Representation in the News Media', in M. Martinelli and T. Judt (eds), *The Politics of Affirmative Action and the Development of a Multicultural Citizenship: Euro–US Perspectives* (New York: Remarque Institute, New York University).

Law, I. and Harrison, M. (1999) 'Positive Action, Particularism and Practice', unpublished working paper, Department of Sociology and Social Policy, University of Leeds.

Law, I. with Henfrey J. (1981) *A History of Race and Racism in Liverpool, 1660–1950* (Liverpool: Merseyside Community Relations Council).

Law, I. with Svennevig, M. and Morrison D. (1997) *Privilege and Silence: 'Race' in the British News during the General Election Campaign* (Leeds: University of Leeds).

Leech, K. (1986) 'Diverse Reports and the Meaning of Racism', *Race and Class*, vol. 28(2), Autumn.

Leicht, K. T. (ed.) (1999) *The Future of Affirmative Action, Research in Social Stratification and Mobility* Vol. 17 (Stamford, Conn.: JAI Press).

Lijphart, A. (1977) *Democracy in Plural Societies: A Comparative Exploration* (New Haven: Yale University Press).

Lloyd, C. (1994) 'Universalism and Difference: The Crisis of Anti-Racism in France and England', in A. Rattansi and S. Westwood (eds), *Racism, Modernity and Identity* (Cambridge: Polity Press).

Lorimer, D.A. (1978) *Colour, Class and the Victorians: English Attitudes and the Negro in the Mid-Nineteenth Century* (Leicester: Leicester University Press).

Lule, J. (1997) 'The Rape of Mike Tyson: Race, the Press and Symbolic Types', in D. Berkowitz, *Social Meanings of News* (London: Sage).

Lustgarten, L. (1992) 'Racial Inequality, Public Policy and the Law: Where Are We Going', in B. Hepple and E. Szyszczak (eds), *Discrimination: The Limits of the Law* (London: Mansell).

Mac an Ghaill, M. (1999) *Contemporary Racism and Ethnicities, Social and Cultural Transformations* (Buckingham: Open University Press).

Mason, D. (1992) 'Some Problems with the Concept of Race and Racism', *Discussion Papers in Sociology*, S92/5 (Leicester: University of Leicester).

McLean, P. (1995) 'Mass Communication, Popular Culture and Racism', in B. Bowler (ed.), *Racism and Anti-Racism in World Perspective* (London: Sage).

McNair, B. (1995) *An Introduction to Political Communication* (London: Routledge).

McNair, B. (1996) *News and Journalism in the UK* (London: Routledge).

McNair, B. (1998) *The Sociology of Journalism* (London: Arnold).

McQuail, D. (1992) *Media Performance: Mass Communication and the Public Interest* (London: Sage).

Mercer, K. (1989) 'General Introduction', in T. Daniels and J. Gerson (eds), *The Colour Black: Black Images on British Television* (London: British Film Institute).

Meyers, M. (1997) *News Coverage of Violence against Women* (London: Sage).

Miles, R. (1989) *Racism* (London: Routledge).

Miller, J. (1997) 'Immigration, the Press and the New Racism', in E. E. Dennis and E. C. Pease (eds), *The Media in Black and White* (New Jersey: Transaction).

Mirza, H.S. (ed.) (1997) *British Black Feminisms* (London: Routledge).

Modood, T. (1996) 'The Changing Context of "Race" in Britain', A Symposium on Anti-Racism, *Patterns of Prejudice*, vol. 30(1), pp. 3–13.

Modood, T. *et al.* (1997) *Ethnic Minorities in Britain, Diversity and Disadvantage* (London: Policy Studies Institute).

Mullan, B. (1996) *Not a Pretty Picture, Ethnic Minority Views of Television* (Aldershot: Avebury).

Mullan, B. (1997) *Consuming Television* (Oxford: Blackwell).

Murdock, G. (1984) 'Reporting the Riots', in J. Benyon (ed.), *Scarman and After* (Oxford: Pergamon).

Murray, N. (1987) 'Reporting the "Riots"', *Race and Class*, vol. 29 (1), Summer.

Murray, N. and Searle, C. (1989) *Racism and the Press in Thatcher's Britain* (London: Institute of Race Relations).

Nazroo, J. (1997) *The Health of Ethnic Minorities in Britain* (London: PSI).

Negrine, R. (1994) *Politics and the Mass Media in Britain*, 2nd edn (London: Routledge).

Ouaj, J. (1998) *More Colour in the Media* (Dusseldorf: European Institute for the Media).

Owens, J. (1999) 'Documentary and Citizenship: The Case of Stephen Lawrence', in J. Stokes and A. Reading (eds), *The Media in Britain, Current Debates and Developments* (London: Macmillan – now Palgrave).

Parekh, B. (1997) 'National Culture and Multiculturalism', in K. Thompson (ed.), *Media and Cultural Regulation* (London: Sage).

Parker, J. (1975) 'Blacks on the Box: Where Are They?', *New Community*, vol. 4(4).

Pease, E.C. (1989) 'Kerner plus 20: Minority News Coverage in the Columbus Dispatch', *Newspaper Research Journal* vol. 10(3), pp. 17–38.

Philo, G. (ed.) (1999) *Message Received* (Harlow: Longman).

Philo, G. and Beattie, L. (1999) 'Race, Migration and Media', in G. Philo (ed.), *Message Received* (Harlow: Longman).

Pines, J. (ed.) (1992) *Black and White in Colour* (London: British Film Institute).

Pitt, G. (1992) 'Can Reverse Discrimination be Justified', in B. Hepple and E. Szyszczak (eds), *Discrimination: The Limits of Law* (London: Mansell).

Rattansi, A. (1994) 'Western Racisms, Ethnicities and Identities in a "Postmodern" Frame', in A. Rattansi and S. Westwood (eds), *Racism, Modernity and Identity* (Cambridge: Polity Press).

Reading, A. (1999) 'Campaigns to Change the Media', in J. Stokes and A. Reading (eds), *The Media in Britain, Current Debates and Developments* (London: Macmillan – now Palgrave).

Riggins, S. (ed.) (1992) *Ethnic Minority Media, an International Perspective* (London: Sage).

Roscoe, W. (1787) *The Wrongs of Africa* (Liverpool).

Roscoe, W. (1788) *A Scriptural Refutation of a Pamphlet Published by the Rev. R. Harris* (Liverpool).

Ross, K. (1992) *Television in Black and White, Ethnic Stereotypes and Popular Television* (Coventry: Centre for Research in Ethnic Relations Research Paper No.19).

Ross, K. (1996) *Black and White Media, Black Images in Popular Film and Television* (Cambridge: Polity Press).

174   *References*

Ross, K. (1997) 'Viewing (P)Leasure, Viewer Pain: Black Audiences and British Television', *Leisure Studies*, vol. 16, pp. 233–48.
Ross, K. (1998) 'Making Race Matter – an Overview', in B. Franklin and D. Murphy (eds), *Making the Local News* (London: Routledge).
Sampson, E. E. (1999) *Dealing with Difference, an Introduction to the Social Psychology of Prejudice* (Fort Worth: Harcourt Brace).
Sato, K. (1997) 'Same Language, Same Race': The Dilemma of Kanbun in Modern Japan', in F. Dikotter (ed.), *The Construction of Racial Identities in China and Japan* (London: Hurst).
Sanderson, F. E. (1976) 'The Liverpool Abolitionists', *Transactions of the Historic Society of Lancashire and Cheshire*, pp. 220–35.
Scobie, E. (1972) *Black Britannia* (Chicago: University of Chicago Press).
Sewell, T. (1997) *Black Masculinity* (Stoke-on-Trent: Trentham).
Seymour-Ure, C. (1996) *The British Press and Broadcasting since 1945* (Oxford: Blackwell).
Shohat, E. and Stam, R. (1994) *Unthinking Eurocentrism: Multiculturalism and the Media* (London: Routledge).
Shyllon, F. O. (1977) *Black Slaves in Britain* (London: Oxford University Press).
Silverstone, R. (1994) *Television and Everyday Life* (London: Routledge).
Snead, J. (1994) *White Screens Black Images: Hollywood from the Dark Side* (London: Routledge).
Solomos, J. and Back, L. (1996) *Racism and Society* (London: Macmillan – now Palgrave).
Spicker, P. (1993/94) 'Understanding Particularism', *Critical Social Policy*, vol. 39 (13), 3, Winter, pp. 5–20.
Statham, P. (1999) 'Political Mobilisation by Minorities in Britain: Negative Feedback of "Race Relations"', *Journal of Ethnic and Migration Studies*, vol. 25(4), October, pp. 597–626.
Stevenson, R.L. and Greene, M.T. (1980) 'A Reconsideration of Bias in the News', *Journalism Quarterly*, vol. 57, pp. 115–21.
Stone, J. (1999) 'Affirmative Action in a Global Context', in M. Martinelli and T. Judt (eds), *The Politics of Affirmative Action and the Development of a Multi-cultural Citizenship: Euro–US perspectives* (New York: Remarque Institute, New York University).
Thompson, K. (ed.) (1997) *Media and Cultural Regulation* (London: Sage/ Open University).
Tronto, J. (1993) *Moral Boundaries* (London: Routledge).
Troyna, B. and Hatcher, R. (1992) *Racism in Children's Lives, a Study of Mainly White Primary Schools* (London: Routledge).
Tumber, H. (1982) *Television and the Riots* (London: British Film Institute).
Turner, B. (1986) *Equality* (London: Tavistock).
Twitchin, J. (ed.) (1988) *The Black and White Media Book* (Stoke on Trent: Trentham).

Valdiva, A. (ed.) (1995) *Feminism, Multiculturalism and the Media* (London: Sage).

Wadsworth, M. (1986) 'Racism in Broadcasting', in J. Curran (ed.), *Bending Reality: The State of the Media, (London: Pluto)*.

Walvin, J. (1971) *The Black Presence: A Documentary History of the Negro in England, 1555–1833* (London: Orbachs & Chambers).

Webster, C. (1995) *Youth Crime, Victimisation and Harassment* (Bradford: Bradford and Ilkley Community College).

Weiner, M. (1997) 'The Invention of Identity: Race and Nation in Pre-war Japan', in F. Dikotter (ed.), *The Construction of Racial Identities in China and Japan* (London: Hurst).

West, C. (1990) 'The New Politics of Cultural Difference', in R. Ferguson, M. Gever, T.T. Minh-ha and C. West (eds), *Out There* (Cambridge, MA: MIT Press), pp. 19–36.

Wheeler, M. (1997) *Politics and the Mass Media* (Oxford: Blackwell).

Williams, P. J. (1997) *Seeing a Colour-Blind Future, The Paradox of Race*, 1997 Reith Lectures (London: Virago).

Wilson, T. (1993) *Watching Television, Hermeneutics, Reception and Popular Culture* (Cambridge: Polity Press).

Wilson, W. J. (1987) *The Truly Disadvantaged: The Inner City, the Underclass and Public Policy* (Chicago: University of Chicago Press).

Wober, J. and Fazal, S. (1984) *Citizens of Ethnic Minorities: Their Prominence in Real Life and on Television* (London: Independent Broadcasting Authority).

Wolfsfeld, G. (1997) *Media and Political Conflict: News from the Middle East* (Cambridge: Cambridge University Press).

Young, L. (1996) *Fear of the Dark: 'Race', Gender, and Sexuality in the Cinema* (London: Routledge).

Index